TEACHING ENGLISH IN ASIA

FINDING A JOB AND DOING IT WELL

GALEN HARRIS VALLE

PACIFIC VIEW PRESS

BERKELEY, CALIFORNIA

Cover design by Rene Yung

ISBN 1-881896-11-0
Library of Congress Catalog Card Number 94-74933
Printed in the United States of America

This book is dedicated to my wife, Amara; my daughter Narissa; and to my mother. I would also like to thank my past, present, and future students for providing the inspiration to put it together.

Contents

Chapter Three: The Student 71

Chapter Four: The Class... 107

Introduction

The primary goal of this text is to shed some light on teaching English in East Asia for those thinking about living and working there. The information and advice are drawn from my experience of more than 15,000 classroom hours as a freelance teacher in East Asia. It is a realistic guide to getting started. It explains where the jobs are, but is not a list of addresses. Address lists are a good way to get started on a job hunt—and therefore some are included in the appendix—but most useful addresses are obtained during the actual job search, not before. The book will also be useful to those who are already teaching, as it offers practical advice that can be effectively used in the EFL classroom.

During my years in several East Asian countries, as an English teacher, teacher trainer, and as the director of a private language center, I have found that teachers who are new to the region often ask the same questions. Experienced teachers often face the same problems as recent arrivals.

I have long felt that many of the textbooks and other teaching materials that I have used were meant for someone else. I have observed that in Asia the most commonly used teaching materials and techniques are geared toward students studying in English-speaking countries (ESL), toward European students, or toward colleagues the writer hopes to impress—but none of my students have fallen into those categories. Many of the opinion-oriented exercises in ESL/EFL texts put Asian students in a quandary: whether to try to please the teacher by attempting to express a strong opinion, or follow cultural norms and remain neutral (at least in public).

Also, many of the topical exercises found in these texts have little relevance to the day-to-day lives of average Asian students. Teachers who are new to teaching in Asia are often perplexed about how materials that proved popular elsewhere could fail miserably when tried in class there. They find that they must first familiarize themselves with what is, and is not, acceptable in Asian societies. Materials can then be chosen that fall within those cultural boundaries. In any given text, some exercises will be fine as they are. Others will have to be adapted or avoided altogether. The last section of this book includes a variety of exercises that have proven popular in many Asian countries, but even these should be selected carefully to fit the needs of each group of students.

Further, although the terms "EFL" (English as a Foreign Language) and "ESL" (English as a Second Language) are often used synonymously, ESL refers to non-native speakers studying English in an English-speaking country, and EFL is for non-native speakers studying in their home country. ESL materials contain localized (USA, UK) information. They often concentrate on "active adaptation" to English-speaking societies, which may not be of interest to many EFL students. Therefore, the EFL instructor should choose materials that will help keep the content of the course consistent with the goals of the students.

With all this in mind, I decided to put together answers to the typical questions, offer suggestions on how to solve common problems, provide an outline of suitable teaching techniques, and help the teacher sift through the huge amount of EFL material and find what is suitable for use in East Asia.

This book is necessarily general. It attempts to cover a vast geographic area and a variety of diverse, complex cultures. The assortment of personalities you will find in class defies generalization. Nevertheless, as a group these individuals do share many characteristics. Therefore, the focus is on what these students have in common rather than what makes them different.

I have used the general term "East Asian student," but done my best throughout to show when generalities do not apply. Likewise, "school," "language center," and "university" (or "college") often come up. The last two terms are used in the traditional sense, while the first could mean any venue in which English is taught—whether a picnic table under a tree, or a prestigious university. Information that applies to specific venues is so indicated.

This book might raise a bit of controversy among ESL theorists, but it was not written for them. It is intended for classroom teachers who spend their time in front of classes of East Asian students. The theories were developed from practice, not vice-versa. I firmly believe that classroom techniques should focus on realistic situations and not be based on what could be possible if a certain number of (often impossible) conditions are met.

A small war is being fought over whether EFL belongs in the realm of academia or of business. Some of those on the academic side, often in "practical" journal articles, take the simple task (it is simple) of teaching EFL and raise it to ludicrous levels of complexity. Conversely, the business side often oversimplifies the role of the teacher: "Just go in there and talk. They will learn something." Wrong. The students are the ones who should be doing the talking, and it takes skill to get them to do that.

Marketing can also cause some confusion among students regarding what "type" of English they should study. The simple fact that English is English is often lost in the diverse marketing tactics used by language schools. "Business English," "Travel English" and various other "kinds" of English are offered. This can also leave teachers at a loss about how to teach terms such as "purchasing power parity" to students who do not know how to say "hello."

The English taught in conversation classes should be varied enough to please the students while remaining within the boundaries of their ability. If possible, they should be made to understand that correctly spoken (and understood) English is viable in all situations when used by all speakers. Topical/thematic courses are merely a means of extending the basic principles taught in conversation classes. Learning a language takes far longer than many students expect (and many advertisements suggest). Patience is essential on both the part of the student and that of the teacher.

I hope that this book will provide insight for those classroom teachers with little or no experience in East Asia regarding what they can expect from their students and what their students will expect from them. More experienced teachers can use the information herein to confirm, explain, or compare with their own experiences and ideas—all with the common goal of making the EFL classroom a more interesting and productive place for both students and teachers.

Galen Harris Valle
Chiang Mai, Thailand

ONE

The Job

Many people are no longer content merely to travel, but want something more from their experience abroad. Travel offers only short-lived contacts. Living abroad requires hands-on participation.

Visitors to East Asia often find that just as they begin to understand the lifestyle and really enjoy themselves, they have to turn around and go home. You don't have to go home. A job teaching English provides a way to stay, to make a living, and to participate.

Economic growth has been spectacular in China, Taiwan, Indonesia, and Thailand in recent years. The ascent that began in the 1970s continues, and the resulting prosperity is providing Asians with ever-expanding opportunities for contact with Westerners. Business, travel, and social interactions are becoming more diversified. With this diversification comes a need for a common medium of communication. Without question, English has filled that need. In East Asia, the use of English is not limited to interactions with Westerners. Asians of different nationalities use English for communication among themselves. In extreme circumstances, it is even used among individuals of similar ethnic origins as a bridge between dialects (e.g., a Hong Kong native and a native of Beijing). Naturally, with the demand for English comes a demand for native-speaking teachers.

These "native speakers" are a varied group. One school where I worked had a staff comprised of a defense attorney, a taxi driver from

Perth, a 65-year-old journalism professor, a political science major, a Ph.D. in linguistics, a computer systems analyst, and a bartender, among others. They were all doing the same job, and they were there for essentially the same reasons. They had differing levels of dissatisfaction with their jobs in the West, and they all had an active interest in East Asia and in teaching. Most schools in the region are similarly staffed.

With the exception of the standard English courses offered at high schools and universities, the "conversation" class is the most popular setting in which East Asians study English. Venues differ with the economy. They can range from posh, air-conditioned classrooms in an urban Japanese high-rise to a rustic fan-cooled room in a Thai wooden house. Wages can run from $40 an hour in Japan to $150 a month in China. But what goes on in these rooms is essentially the same. Teachers of conversation are expected to teach their students to speak and understand the language so that it can be used in everyday life—with little emphasis on grammar other than that which is necessary for successful communication. In TEFL (Teaching English as a Foreign Language) parlance, this is called the "communicative approach."

Conversation classes are generally taught at privately owned language centers. They are most frequently attended by high-school and university students from upper-income families. They are also popular with adults from 25 to 35 years of age, and the number of children from 8 to 12 is increasing fast. Few middle-aged people attend, although it is not unusual to find a parent and child in the same school, or maybe even the same class. The oldest student I ever encountered was about 70—the same age as the oldest EFL teacher I ever met (in Laos). All will have studied English in school, so you don't have to start from scratch. But their ability to use the language is minimal (remember high-school French class?).

Not long ago, when English was considered to be more of a novelty than a necessity, it was possible for a Westerner of any nationality to obtain a teaching position almost anywhere in East Asia by simply being Occidental. For example, a German who could speak almost no English walked into a job teaching in Indonesia and learned as he went. He became fluent after several years, along with his loyal students, and is still teaching today.

The increase in independent travel to East Asia since the early 1980s has glutted the market for "walk in off the street" teaching. It has become a buyer's market, and is limited to fly-by-night operations often located near "traveler's centers," the inexpensive guest-house areas listed in every guidebook on independent Asian travel. "Teacher Wanted— No Experience Necessary [sic]" signs are often posted on the bulletin boards of larger guest-houses and hostels. These sign-posting schools generally, but not always, pay their teachers at the end of each day and are just as likely as not to be closed when the teacher (or student) reports to the next class. (Note: schools typically use signs on bulletin boards to advertise job vacancies, but legitimate schools usually advertise at universities and bicultural centers—*not* guest houses.)

At legitimate language centers, the criteria have become stricter. That does not mean that every teacher needs an advanced degree in applied linguistics. It does mean, however, that one no longer finds too many Western, non-native speakers of English standing at the blackboard, nor does one encounter a lot of down-and-out tourists whose resumés were written on the cover of their last pack of traveler's checks.

There are four ways to get a job teaching EFL in East Asia: (1) apply in person; (2) answer an advertisement; (3) use a commercial recruiter, or (4) join a volunteer program. A fifth method, for which the chances of success are almost negligible, is to send letters of application randomly to schools in a selected area.

Most schools that recruit teachers from abroad take care of everything, including legal requirements, for the teacher. This is a convenience, and these schools may even offer round-trip transportation as a perk. Nevertheless, be aware that most perks for those hired from abroad come with a price. Salaries for these teachers are often substantially lower than those paid to instructors hired locally, and contracts often forbid teaching at other venues.

Although beginning teachers might feel more comfortable setting up a job in advance, experienced teachers know that a speculative job search is always more lucrative. If you are attracted by the thought of working in the rural settings offered by volunteer programs like WorldTeach that pay next to nothing, go to a small town, find something that looks like a school, and tell the people there that you want to teach. This will save you the $3,000 recruiter's fee, and you are left free to accept any other jobs you find. This additional employment may make the difference between struggling to survive on a pittance or living comfortably on a local scale. A decent income can realistically be achieved in larger towns with regional universities, colleges, or technical schools. These schools might have the budget to take on a foreign teacher, whereas a village or small- town school might not. Additional work could come from businesses and private students in the area. This arrangement would locate you close enough to villages to do some volunteer teaching when time allows. If there are no jobs in the town you have chosen, move on to the next.

Volunteer programs (Peace Corps, WorldTeach, etc.) perform valuable services for Asian peoples in rural areas, and are an excellent way to gain maximum contact with those cultures in a short time. They are not, however, suitable for freelance EFL teachers trying to maximize teaching hours and make a good living.

If the approximately $25,000 a year offered by commercial recruiting programs (TESL Recruiting Service, ELS International, etc.) for teaching jobs in Tokyo sounds good, go there yourself and make $35,000. I estimate that less than 10 percent of teachers in East Asia obtain positions through commercial recruiters. In ten years, I have met about a dozen, and most of them were in Japan.

Job Listings

The best printed source of information on teaching jobs worldwide is the listing of job vacancies published six times a year by TESOL (TESOL Inc., 1600 Cameron St., Suite 300, Alexandria, VA 22314). This vacancy listing should not be confused with the *TESOL Bulletin,* which is a quarterly journal. The best source of names and addresses of schools is the telephone directory of the city in which you are interested (some large Western libraries have these). An excellent source of general information on living and working abroad is *Transitions Abroad* magazine (P.O. Box 344, Amherst, MA 01001).

The most productive places for beginners to focus a speculative job search are large cities in Northeast Asia (Taipei, Tokyo, Seoul). The demand for teachers there is so much higher than the supply that you can be confident of finding work in EFL—although it will take some time to get sufficient teaching hours. The demand is not as high in Southeast Asia, and there is more competition for jobs. Teaching outside of cities there requires some experience (or stubbornness) since you will probably have to initiate every aspect of your employment. A town might have sufficient need for a Western teacher, but no experience in accommodating one. You will have to create your own job either by promoting yourself and setting up your own classroom or by putting together such a great program that the head of a local school will find it irresistible.

Legality

Generally there are two statuses for teachers in East Asia: legal and semi-legal. There is much red tape in either case, and you may not always be sure which category you fall into at any given time.

Legal teaching involves work permits and work visas that usually cannot be arranged by an individual, but rather by most government schools and some private ones. A work permit is generally only valid for work at the institution that arranges it—it is not blanket permission to work anywhere you wish. If you work at a university and a language center, the language center job could well be considered illegal.

Outside of universities, most teaching jobs in East Asia are landed by applying in person to the school, and most of these jobs are "semi-legal."

"Semi-legal" teaching is the reason that information regarding employment in Asia is inconsistent and often unreliable. In theory, it is illegal for any foreign national to work in any country without the appropriate governmental permission. Exceptions, however, exist in many countries for those who can take positions that cannot be filled by locals. English teachers fall into that category. The problem is that the criteria for "a position that cannot be filled by a local" is vague and open to numerous interpretations. When the national government is forced to crack down on foreign factory personnel working illegally, it may also be forced to crack down on foreign teachers simply because they are also foreign nationals working without government permission.

Laws in most parts of East Asia are enforced by "crackdowns." One month the target may be gangsters, the next it may be unlicensed drivers, and the next it may be foreign teachers. I have seen police raids on language schools in some countries, and have also taught at police stations, at a labor office, and to groups of immigration officials during crackdowns. It is anyone's guess as to what could happen when authorities decide to get tough.

In general, in order to teach, if you do not hold a work permit (or work visa):

- ◆ You will need a non-tourist visa. A non-immigrant, business, or other type of visa will be necessary for any work.
- ◆ You will need to pay taxes in order to extend your visa and/or to leave the country.
- ◆ You will be considered a part-time rather than a full-time employee.
- ◆ You will need to leave the country periodically on "visa runs" as do many foreign residents who do not work.
- ◆ You will need to keep your visa in perfect order (no overstays) to ensure that you are allowed back in the country.

Many language centers operate via loopholes as do teachers who work semi-legally and do not officially exist in the eyes of the government regarding their employment as teachers. (Note: "loophole" here connotes an exception due to social position, social connections, or family influence. Rules and regulations are enforced arbitrarily in most Asian societies; a loophole in the sense of a "legal oversight" is irrelevant—except immigration regulations, which do not directly affect locals and are more clearcut.) These language centers are not registered businesses, so they cannot officially hire anyone. This is not the mark of a fly-by-night business. In East Asia, registration of a small business (even if it happens to have 30 classrooms and a staff of 40 foreign teachers) is the exception, not the rule. Exceptions are Japan, Korea, and Singapore (*everything* is registered in Singapore), where most schools are registered and work permits are required.

It is usually the responsibility of employers to arrange work permits for those they hire, but permits usually come after one lands a job, not before. Many teachers seek out jobs that offer work permits because of the long-term visa that often accompanies them. Some schools may not make all the arrangements, but they will supply a letter verifying employment, and tell you how to go about applying. If nobody at a particular school has work permits, you don't need one. If everybody has one, so will you. Go with the flow.

In any case, there is little personal risk. No matter what the legal situation is in theory, language schools require governmental permission (although it may be "unofficial" permission) to operate, and they will have the situation well in hand. They will be able to offer the appropriate guidance when it comes to visas, permits, permissions, documentation and so forth.

Legal Maneuvers

Here is an illustration of roundabout legal machinations in Taiwan in the mid 1980s. Most language centers were not registered, so teachers were on their own when it came to visas. In order to extend a visa, one had to go to the tax office, report earnings, pay taxes (about 6 percent of reported income), and get a tax receipt. The tax receipt was then taken to the local police station and presented to police to obtain an extension. Along with the tax receipt (solid proof of a job) one had to state that one was not employed, and present documentation of nonemployment (usually in the form of a letter from a Chinese language school—which was often the same language school where one did in fact work) to prove it. Contradictory, but nobody seemed to notice. Although more schools are registered now and able to supply work permits, things are still generally done the same way.

If it seems peculiar that an unregistered business that doesn't officially exist can obtain unofficial official sanction to operate and hire dozens of teachers who also don't exist, I can only say, "Welcome to East Asia!"

Money

Western EFL teachers in Asia are sometimes publicly accused (usually through letters or op-ed in newspapers) of being opportunists who are only interested in making piles of money and bleeding the economy. In fact, only the most economically developed East Asian countries offer salaries high enough to justify those accusations, and even then only the short-term, get-the-money-and-run types are guilty (although it's not clear what there is to be guilty of, since it's perfectly legal). With the right job connections, for example, one could easily go to Japan, work for six months while living frugally, and leave with more than $10,000. That is regarded as bleeding the economy, and some travelers are able to finance perpetual trips that way. Nevertheless, teaching

English in East Asia is generally not nearly so lucrative as in places like the Middle East, where teachers contract for a set period of time, spend little locally, and return home with substantial savings. Most teachers in East Asia make it there and spend it there.

Wages

Approximate hourly wage (in language centers) in five East Asian countries.*

Japan	$25–$40 per hour
Korea	$20–$35 per hour
Taiwan	$20–$30 per hour
Indonesia	$10–$20 per hour
Thailand	$15 per hour

The wages above do not represent maximum and minimum. They are provided as a basis of comparison.

The Freelance Philosophy

Every English teacher, except full-time university staff, directors, and teacher trainers at language centers, and those stuck in recruitment contracts, is freelance. A freelance attitude is necessary to make a living, as few full-time positions are available; these are reserved for only the most experienced or qualified teachers (or those who happened to be in the right place at the right time).

This is actually a good setup, because part-time teachers generally make more money than their full-time colleagues. They have more control over their schedules, can teach at more places, and can maximize teaching hours.

It is impossible for a freelance English teacher to think in terms of annual, or even monthly, salary. Freelance teachers think in terms of "hours." "How many hours did you get?" is the question teachers ask each other at the beginning of a term. "About how many hours can I expect?" is the question to ask language centers when applying for jobs. The answer to, "How many hours do you work?" is a good way to judge the job market in a new town.

If you could work 40 hours a week, 11 months a year, in Taiwan (where pay rates are high), you would make about $30,000. In Thailand (where pay rates are low), you would make about $20,000. Such earnings are only possible if you are able to work at high-paying venues and keep hours working for low pay (teachers often accept lower-paying work during "non-peak" hours) to a minimum. Teachers who depend on one school for work, or who work during peak teaching times for low pay don't make half that. Most teachers work about six hours a day, with a few hours added on the weekends. It is a struggle to keep those hours up year round.

Approximate Monthly Budget for a Single-Income Family with One Child in Thailand

2-bedroom house in the suburbs	$200
Food and household expenses	350
Gas (1 motorcycle)	5
Water	8
Electricity (1 A/C)	16
Misc. Expenses	20
Entertainment	50
Total	**$649**

One would need to work about 16 hours a week, every week, to cover typical expenses at the average $10-an-hour pay rate in most Thai cities (pay rates and living expenses are higher in Bangkok than in the table above). Many people spend more or less. A single room can rent for about $40 a month near a university, and those with frugal eating habits (cheap food stalls) could spend as little as $120. The food costs above are based on cooking a combination of Thai and Western food (ingredients are often expensive) at home. There is no ceiling when it comes to rent. A one-bedroom apartment in a high-rent district of Bangkok could rent for $2,000 a month while a comparable apartment in a middle-income area could rent for $200.

Approximate Monthly Individual Budget in Taiwan:

1-bedroom urban apartment	$200
Food	200
Gas (1 motorcycle)	10
Water	8
Electricity (1 A/C)	18
Entertainment	150
Total	**$586**

To cover the above budget shown for Taiwan one would have to teach about eight hours a week. The rent is typical for an apartment near a university (students also pay that amount, but will cram six people into the unit). Everyday food is not expensive, but there is no ceiling. Dinner for two at a posh restaurant could easily cost $100. To live cheaper than this in Taiwan would be monastic.

The cost of "visa runs" needs to be added (once a year in Taiwan, and about four times a year in Thailand) to both of these budgets for those who do not hold work permits or resident visas. The cost of these depends on one's travel tastes.

Most urban schools in East Asia (except China) generally offer reasonable hourly rates. Otherwise nobody would be teaching there. Those who work more earn more. Maximizing work hours requires teaching at several locations, organizing your time well, and keeping a sharp lookout for additional jobs. More time is usually spent haggling over hours and class times than over wages. Rates at schools are usually set and pay scales are clearly defined.

The goal is to get to the point where you often have to turn down work, and where you will only accept private students at maximum local pay rates. Many new teachers undercut standard rates because they are desperate for hours. It is always best to charge the highest fair rate possible. For example, I charge similar rates to all private students and explain that the rate is the same for one student or 50 (if they want to economize by having more students share the expense).

Where the Jobs Are:
Private Language Centers

By far the most common source of employment for Westerners, these schools offer higher wages, smaller classes, and more freedom for other pursuits than do universities or other schools. They can range from small one-room affairs in small towns to huge complexes with dozens of rooms and thousands of students in major cities like Tokyo, Taipei, and Bangkok. Most of these schools offer primarily conversation classes in English and Japanese, although some specialize in university entrance-exam preparation and only offer English conversation as a sideline.

There is no need to pay attention to the names of these centers, which are often the same or similar to those of well-known international language institutes. Some are authorized branches, others are not. In Taiwan, companies can only register their names within a limited area. Or, more likely, the company does not register at all. A school in Taipei (northern Taiwan) may have the same name and a similar logo to that of a school in Taichung (central Taiwan) although there is no actual affiliation.

Borrowing names is common among Asian businesses, and a name that lacks originality is no indication of a shady enterprise, as might be the case in the West. Unscrupulous schools are now rare outside of "traveler's centers" because of competition from legitimate schools that offer higher quality instruction, and the advent of rising consumer education and awareness in East Asia.

Careful research is important when choosing a school, and other teachers are the best source of information on a given city. Some teachers, however, may be reluctant to share information—especially if there is a shortage of classes. Job searches necessitate much legwork and some learning from experience when it comes to judging the character of schools.

The easiest way by far to land a job is to have a recommendation from a present (or former) staff member or even just the name of one to mention to the curriculum director.

Alternatively, if you observe a school around 6 p.m. and see a lot of students and teachers roaming around, it is probably worth returning during a less hectic part of the day to discuss applying for a position.

The best time to apply is during the afternoon when the staff is less busy. Arriving five minutes before the 6 p.m. class of a new term will not only result in a refusal, but in not even being noticed in the chaos. Mornings are also bad because those responsible for interviews usually don't arrive until later, and it can be frustrating to deal with a non-English-speaking secretary whose job is to assist students rather than prospective teachers. A job hunt should also be timed so that it does not coincide with examination dates at local universities and local holidays. Enrollment is low during these times, and it is far better to apply during the summer (or dry season in Southeast Asia) when enrollment is at its peak.

Some language centers like a resumé to accompany applications, while others are mostly interested in personality, and the information on the application form is sufficient. Some schools require a written test, and others even demand a "teaching demonstration" in which staff members act as students.

A telephone number where you can be reached is essential when job hunting, but be warned that applications on which the contact number is that of a guest house or other transient accommodation often go to the bottom of the pile.

Keep in mind that the only time anyone is going to be hired is when someone is needed. One person may try unsuccessfully for weeks for a job at a particular school while another may happen to walk in just as a class of 20 people has enrolled and all the existing staff members are unavailable. If someone who seems qualified is already there, the curriculum director can obviously save time and effort by hiring that person.

Some fly-by-night schools request an application fee as a way of making extra income. Don't pay it. There is no possibility of being hired in these centers (what staff they have is generally local). Avoid them.

Getting Hired: The Interview
Interviewing for EFL teaching jobs can be different from interviewing for jobs in other fields. The interviewer could be an Asian or a Westerner—the degree of experience of either in each other's

respective societies will strongly affect the tone of the interview. However, both will want to see an energetic, well-dressed, open-minded applicant who, hopefully, has some experience in the field. It is helpful if that experience has been gained in the country where the interview is taking place. Long experience in China, for example, may not impress someone in Thailand. Nevertheless, experience in an Asian country is far more relevant than experience in a European one, and of course some experience anywhere is better than none at all. These preferences are, however, easily disregarded if there is an open position with few or no qualified applicants.

An interview with a Westerner can be straightforward and much like that for a teaching job at home. But an interviewer can seem arrogant and cynical regarding an applicant's teaching—and in-country—experience. Some Westerners who have been living and working long-term in Asia feel that one could not possibly have any idea about how things operate unless one has spent a significant amount of time (perhaps ten years or more) living—not just traveling—in that country. And the number of short-term tourists/independent travelers who apply for jobs in Asian cities is overwhelming to many language center directors.

There is also an "Old Boy Network." People who know the right people, or were at the right place at the right time, receive preferential treatment: "Oh! You were working in Beijing during the Tiananmen Square protest? So was I! Did you know Paul? Yeah . . . well he's in Tokyo now . . . might be here in a few months? Sit down, have some coffee. How many hours did you want?"

But most interviewers simply want to separate those who are truly interested from transients who will, in most cases, leave after only a few weeks and damage the reputation of the school by doing so. (All interviewers, however, realize that most people won't stay around for years—and they won't pay much attention to those who state that they plan to.) The worst possible way to start an interview with many Westerners would be to say something like "I've been traveling in Asia for about eight months now, and . . . " or to put something like "extensive travel in Indonesia" on a job application. Transient "teachers" are also responsible for the unpopular policy at some legitimate schools of holding back a month's pay in order to encourage people to stay.

When I was the director of a language center in Thailand, I didn't supply application forms or ask questions. If applicants came in with a stack of diplomas and certificates, the documents were pointedly ignored.

I listened to them talk. If they said something like, "I taught in Indonesia for a couple years," I would press for details: names of schools, streets, and people. It was easy to tell if they were being truthful. More could be learned about a teacher's ability and experience in a five-minute conversation than from the most detailed resumé. Few directors have as much faith in first impressions as I do, but I rarely had problems with teachers.

Interviews with Asians can also be straightforward if the interviewer has had some experience living abroad or has been working with Westerners for a long time. At other times, they can be extremely misleading.

A teacher who had been working in Taiwan for a couple of years at a university went to an interview for a part-time, evening job at a language center. The director was impressed that the candidate had been working in the country for two years (quite the opposite of how a Western interviewer might react). He convinced the teacher that a full-time teaching position at his language school would be more rewarding than the position the teacher already held, both financially and academically, because the classes were smaller and the pay was higher. The director assured him that he could start full-time at the beginning of the next term when a very high enrollment was expected. The teacher noted that if he resigned from the university where he was teaching his work permit would be invalid, and the director assured him that things would be taken care of. After further discussion, they reached an agreement that the teacher would resign from his university position and begin employment on a given date.

During the interim, the teacher made several visits to the school, and was well received by the director, taken to dinner a few times, and assured that he had made the right decision.

The teacher reported to work on the appointed day only to find there was no job waiting for him. The director had instead given the job to an American classmate of his son's who would be coming to Taiwan specifically for that purpose. After some argument, and seeing himself in an untenable situation, the teacher left. To look for work. The university had already replaced him. This story ends with the friend of the director's son also looking for work; the projected high enrollment never materialized.

This story is typical, and it exemplifies how cultural differences can cause unexpected problems when two individuals from different cultural backgrounds expect each other to operate on the same set of social ethics. The director probably saw nothing wrong in doing a favor for his son and did not feel guilty because his expectations fell short. He may have even been a bit offended that the teacher would argue about a simple change in plans. The Western teacher, on the other hand, must have felt that he was treated unfairly (according to his own ethics), and that the director was morally wrong in his seeming disregard of their agreement.

Promises made during job interviews can be based only on what the interviewer "hopes" will happen, and not on what actually "will" happen. Such promises are made at one time or another to nearly every teacher anywhere in Asia. Unfortunately, people often act on these promises, giving up current employment for promised employment at another venue.

Western interviewers are often clearer about terms than their Asian colleagues are, sometimes clarifying that the job under discussion is only a possibility.

Many Asian societies traditionally tend to put all human relationships into set categories. (Five are outlined in the *Book of Mencius:* between sovereign and subject, between father and son, between husband and wife, between brothers, between friends.) There is no place in the scheme of things for a relationship between employer and applicant. Promises made in the context of a non-relationship are considered to be nothing more than standard politeness to strangers, while a promise to someone who enjoys one of these recognized relationships can be considered an obligation (there are also varying views of what constitutes an "obligation"). In the above case, however, the promise made to the son did not work out either—although the son was not directly affected. The only two people who really lost anything were the two teachers—with whom the director had no proper relationship.

The thoughts of Mencius are archaic, but aspects of the "five relationships" still apply, although many people might not realize that these values are embedded in a concept that was considered dated by some even when it was introduced over two millennia ago.

Although the "five relationships" is a Chinese concept, elements of it can be found in other Asian societies, and Asians affected by it often fail to recognize how different it can be from Western expectations in business relations.

The only reasonable plan of action under these circumstances would be to go along with the offer and "promise" to take the job—while still making no plans to stop any current undertakings. Only if there is solid proof of the new position should other commitments be canceled. This may seem irresponsible and sure to cause hard feelings with the old employer, but it is a common situation. Most employers in Asia are used to it, realizing that they would do exactly the same in this situation. Of course employees are expected to perform competently, but if a better opportunity presents itself, few employers will object or stand in the way of your departure.

Don't give too much credence to promises about possible forthcoming jobs. The curriculum director's (or whoever is doing the hiring) highest priority is to be sure that every class has a teacher otherwise he or she may have to assume the task. Directors are not above stringing applicants along in order to keep them in reserve. It is impossible for a director to know how many students will enroll for a term beginning in a few weeks, and until the time tuition is actually paid, the numbers are pure guesswork. If a school cannot offer a class within a week or two (or by the next term), move on.

This is why it is usually a waste of time to send a written application to a language center. Even if a reply is sent, it will be along the lines of, "We would love to talk to you when you are in town." The only way a director can tell if someone has the right personality for teaching conversation is to talk to that individual face-to-face.

Getting Enough Work

Conversation classes at most private language centers are usually small (8 to 15 students). The most popular time for study (and thus the greatest need for teachers) is in the early evening. The morning ranks second in popularity, and it is also possible for new teachers to find work then.

Freelance Class Schedule

The following is an example of a schedule in mid-1994 in Chiang Mai, Thailand.

University Classes ($6 per hour)

M/W/F	T/Th
8:00–9:00 a.m.	8:00–9:30 a.m.
11:00–12:00 a.m.	11:00–12:30 p.m.
1:00–2:00 p.m.	

Language Center ($9 per hour)

5:00–8:00 p.m.	5:00–8:00 p.m.

Private Tutorials ($12 per hour)

9:00–10:00	9:00–12:00

(39 hours per week: 15 hrs @ $6 + 15 hours @ $9 + 9 hours @ $12 = $333 per week; $1332 per month.)

Teachers are also often needed for "one-by-one" classes for individual students at odd hours. These classes often pay slightly less (or more, depending on the venue) than regular classes.

The initial workload of a new teacher typically will be one or two evening classes. It is rare that a new teacher is given more than that without having proved his or her abilities, and a few hours in the evening may be all a school can offer. If so, you should find another school for morning work, a third for afternoons, and fill odd hours with private students. Peak times vary with the venue. Children's schools often need instructors in the afternoon (a dead time at most adult centers). Schools are often more agreeable about scheduling class times if you are "in demand" (already working) than they are when they know you need them. I once taught at three schools in the same building.

At most centers, classes are one to one and a half hours and are held Monday through Friday; Monday, Wednesday, and Friday; or Tuesday and Thursday. The less frequently the class meets, the longer the classes will be. At some centers, marathon weekend classes running three to five hours a day are possible.

Seniority is important. Senior teachers are given first choice for hours, and the new teachers take what is left over. Most centers have a core staff of a few teachers who have been there several years. The turnover rate for other staff members is high. Gaining enough seniority to rate sufficient hours does not take too long.

Once you have one class, the key to getting more is re-enrollment. The owners of most language centers are business people, not academics. Teachers whose students re-enroll for further classes are considered to be valuable assets, and they receive high priority when teaching hours are allotted.

A private language center is an excellent venue for spontaneously using what you learn about your students to their benefit without being hampered by the confines of a strict syllabus. Most language centers do require the use of a textbook, but a good teacher is generally given a free hand in using it.

Many teachers who opt to work at universities may find themselves working evenings at a private language center as an escape from syllabus tedium or simply to make extra money. You should make it a point to visit the centers in your area even if you are not actively seeking employment. A teacher who is employed elsewhere and stops by to chat will be remembered in the future if he or she applies for a job.

Other Jobs: Universities and Colleges

Universities are generally more demanding about credentials than language centers, although the pay for part-timers is often lower than in private centers. Full-time teaching positions at large universities are usually arranged through academic channels and set up in advance.

Classes are large and a strict syllabus is used—or the teacher will be required to write one. Texts for university classes are commonly staff written, and they can range from good to terrible. Much more emphasis is placed on vocabulary and grammar than on the speaking and listening that is stressed at private language centers.

In many East Asian universities in recent years, good locally produced (or adapted) instructional materials have become available. Although they are still rare, these materials can be more closely matched with the needs of local students than materials available elsewhere—you might even "borrow" some of them for use in other classes outside the university.

Vocational colleges and secondary schools in Asia are now starting to offer English courses taught by Western teachers. Many of these programs are in their infancy and have not yet developed syllabi. In some cases, reference materials are not even available, and teachers are expected to "wing it" or even develop a syllabus on their own time. Because preparing courses can involve long hours for little or no compensation, these schools are an alternative for those who are not trying to maximize hours, those with their own teaching materials, or those who are willing make the effort to find schools with a viable program to duplicate.

Although the salary is on the low end, around 40 percent less per hour than language centers, work at universities is steady. Classes do not have to depend on popularity trends as private language centers do. At universities, vacation times are planned and sometimes even paid, and there is no anxiety about whether there will be enough students to fill your classes next term. Part-time work at universities, colleges, and secondary schools can also help fill those slack morning and afternoon hours. But be prepared to spend extra time proctoring and grading exams, and keeping (often unpaid) office hours for student consultations. Some teachers choose universities because they offer assistance with visas and work permits that many language centers cannot.

University positions are also suitable for those who are interested in working in addition to studying, or who are seeking practical experience in formal teaching. Teaching university classes can also lead to higher paying, private tutorials if the classes are well received (students often expect their teachers to offer "extra" classes for which payment is arranged privately).

Before accepting a teaching position at a college, secondary school, or university, clearly understand what is expected of teachers by the powers-that-be. Also, carefully check textbooks and other materials for comprehensiveness and authenticity.

Many teachers find experience at universities and colleges to be rewarding if they have taken the time to find the right school with a program that fits their abilities, expectations, and schedule.

Working for Private Companies

Travel agencies, hotels, airlines, banks, factories, import/export companies, insurance companies, and many other businesses are a viable source of employment for English teachers.

Hotels that offer programs for their staffs sometimes provide instructors with room and board in addition to a moderate salary. Some hotels have their own EFL programs, while others have the teacher design the courses.

It is also possible to teach at hotels on an hourly basis as part of your freelance teaching schedule. When freelancing, it is essential to convey to hotel management that they are not your employer, but your client. You should make the decisions regarding pay rate, schedule, and most other aspects of your services. Otherwise "extra work" requested by hotel management can be a burden. This requires a lot of negotiation, plus a realistic awareness that hotel managers are often very shrewd and rarely give something for nothing.

When applying for a teaching position at a hotel, whether as a "house" teacher or freelancer, provide a resumé of related work experience along with separate course outlines for the Reception/Public Relations staff and the Food and Beverage staff. The English level of the former is generally far higher than that of the latter, and each group will need to be taught separately. These course outlines show that you have given some thought to what you plan to teach. In many cases, the hotel management will opt to use your program even if they already have one of their own.

Once, after submitting an application to a hotel for a teaching job, I was offered a management job—although I had no experience in that field. Hotels sometimes find in English teachers what they want in managers. (I didn't accept the position, but others do take such employment.)

Care should be given to the style and content of all application and course outline materials submitted to a hotel. The English ability of the personnel and management staff who will review the application could range from excellent to nonexistent. Use language that is clear, simple, and natural regardless of whether the person who reviews the application is a native English-speaker or English-speaking local.

Many other businesses provide after-hours English classes for their employees, or will consider doing so if the teacher presents a well-thought-out topical/thematic course outline for consideration.

Other Employment Options

Once you gain a reasonable amount of practical experience, you may grow tired of the grind and pollution that comes with living in large Asian cities. Fortunately, even the smallest town has opportunities for teaching, and it is possible to set yourself up almost anywhere as the resident native-speaking English teacher. Be prepared to ask for lower fees in small towns, as the "Asian economic miracle" may not have reached them yet. Nevertheless, the more relaxed pace and the lower cost of living in small towns can often make up for what is lost in salary.

Country-by-Country Guidelines

The following list is a general look at teaching conditions in various East-Asian countries in terms of legality, availability, salary, and other conditions. Since all conditions are in a constant state of change, they should be used only as a general reference.

But here is a general outline of how things stand at the time of this writing (1995).

Indonesia

Indonesian schools offer higher salaries and more perks than those in any other country in Southeast Asia. It is not difficult to maximize hours, and some urban schools are large enough that they can offer freelancers sufficient hours to make additional jobs optional, rather than necessary.

As usual, universities and other schools pay less than private language centers. They do, however, assist with visas and related immigration requirements—as do some larger language centers that recruit abroad. Other language centers are not in a position to assist with visas, and teachers will have to leave the country every couple of months (these "visa runs," usually to Singapore, are sometimes paid for by the language center). Indonesian immigration officials can be strict with individuals who have dozens of entry stamps in their passports, so it is necessary to "put on your best face" and control your temper if you spend a lot of time running in and out of the country.

Many of the EFL teachers in Indonesia are from Australia or New Zealand. Australians have minimal entry requirements as vacationing Australians provide much of Indonesia's tourism income. New Zealand has a reciprocal agreement with ASEAN countries that allows its nationals an automatic two- or three-month stay generally on entry (no visa). Other native English-speakers are also in demand, and work is not difficult to find.

Schools in Jakarta and its suburbs offer the highest salaries. Perks could include "visa runs," comfortable lodging with a housekeeper and night watchman, and paid holidays.

It is advisable to invest time applying in person and shopping around for the best salary and benefits—a certain amount of bargaining should take place if a school is obviously in need of teachers. A second choice would be to contact one of the schools that recruit abroad—ELS International (see Korea listing) has branches on Java. Schools that recruit abroad pay a commission to someone somewhere, and therefore applying in person eliminates the middleman, and the resultant savings to the school should be reflected in your salary. Inquiries by personal letter often receive noncommittal replies.

The combination of high salaries and the low cost of living in Jakarta can go a long way toward making up for the city's obvious deficiencies (overpopulation, pollution, theft, etc.). Yogyakarta is also popular among teachers, and teaching jobs are available on Bali, but very much in demand. Pay rates can drop sharply outside of major cities on Java, and the farther afield you go—there are about 1,400 islands to choose from—the lower salaries will be. If you stray too far from the cities, you will be doing volunteer work.

Indonesian students are often more serious about learning than those in the more affluent Asian countries where studying English is sometimes no more than a pastime or a good excuse to stay out late. Because the majority of your Indonesian students will be Moslems, use appropriate teaching materials that they will not find religiously or culturally offensive. Indonesia also has some internal conflicts (East Timor) and taboos (Chinese communism) that are best to avoid discussing in class.

Thailand

Teaching positions are available at private language centers, universities, vocational schools, and high schools. Private language centers generally pay the highest wages. Although the pay in Thailand does not compare well with the rates in other East Asian countries, the low (but quickly rising) cost of living can make up for it.

Schools in Bangkok pay the highest rates in the country. However, if you are teaching at several locations in Bangkok, be prepared to spend about 30% of your time in transit between classes—especially if you must depend on public transportation. Also, be ready for an indifferent reception at most schools when applying for jobs as there are many Western, casual job seekers in Thailand. The key to being noticed is to have some experience and a healthy dose of the right attitude (see page 43). Be persistent (but not too much so) and check back with schools to which you have applied. Thai universities have two semesters (June to October and November to March). Apply a few weeks before the beginning of a semester as applications submitted any later will be filed— perhaps never to see light again. You must hold an undergraduate degree, at least, and you will be expected to submit a copy upon application along with related documentation and a health certificate (available at low cost from any private medical clinic).

Universities and other government schools arrange work permits and long-term visas—a very lengthy process. The work permit only allows employment at the school that arranges it.

Language centers can legally hire teachers as temporary employees only if they hold non-immigrant visas. Those holding tourist visas cannot be considered. The proper visa can be obtained at any Thai embassy. A double-entry visa is best because it saves a trip to the embassy on the second entry.

Non-immigrant visas are good for a three-month stay, and, although theoretically extensions are not permitted, they can be requested if there is a good reason. This application will take a month or so to be denied, and you are, of course, allowed to remain in the country during the interim.

Some schools deduct taxes and others leave it up to the individual to pay. In any case, a tax number should be applied for and taxes paid at the tax office (you may even get a refund) as a tax receipt is needed to extend work permits.

Regulations regarding foreigners residing in Thailand are currently being reviewed and revised. In mid-1994, immigration officials were strictly regulating issuance and extension of visas for long-term residents. Some individuals leaving the country are being refused visas to reenter, and there is talk of limiting all visas to an extendable one-month stay. This is reportedly an effort to "keep track" of "criminal elements" from other Asian countries. It does, however, affect English teachers more than most other groups of expatriates. It is likely that the current problems are procedural and caused by misunderstandings and misinterpretations of policies that have not been fully instituted. Check with the Thai Embassy for current details.

Taiwan

Taiwan is one of the main areas in East Asia in which English is extensively studied, and pay rates are among the highest. Compensation at universities is low in Taiwan compared to language centers. Universities frequently hire overseas through university work/study programs. Those who work at universities may well find a clause in their contract that forbids outside work and could subsequently find themselves at a financial dead end while others are doing well. This is not an issue for Western students in Taiwan, who are not totally dependent on income from teaching, but it can affect the freelance teacher who is trying to maximize hours. Some comparative shopping regarding salaries is advisable before accepting a teaching job at a university.

Language centers are usually large and offer good wages because they compete with each other to attract teachers. Some language centers recruit from overseas, but teachers hired locally are generally offered a higher hourly pay rate. Conversation classes are the most popular with students. TOEFL preparation classes—often quite large—offering substantially higher pay are available. Those who want to teach TOEFL should familiarize themselves with the test (Barrons and Longman both publish study guides). Landing a class involves competing with very well-qualified local teachers.

American English is preferred in Taiwan, probably owing to the strong influence of the United States. In the past, "Americans" with strong British or Australian accents were common; these temporary changes of nationality are no longer necessary, and non-American English-speakers generally have little trouble finding work.

While finding jobs at Taipei's dozens of language centers is not hard, those who are interested in working long-term may want to look elsewhere on the island, as Taipei is also the destination of many transient teachers, and working conditions often reflect that (many guidebooks suggest a stint teaching in Taiwan as a good way for travelers to make extra money). Some schools hold back a month's pay, and starting salaries can be lower than those of teachers who have been around for a while.

Taiwan does not host many Western tourists, and English is not widely spoken outside of business areas (hence the need for English teachers). Daily activities get much easier as soon as one begins to learn some Mandarin. Many of the teachers in Taiwan are Chinese-language students. There was a huge influx of these students following the Tiananmen Square incident in the People's Republic of China (PRC) in 1989. The number remains high.

Visas to Taiwan are good for two months, and are extendable twice, with each extension requiring visits to the tax office and the main police station in your city of residence. A tax card is necessary for the extension, which is granted by the police. The police will require an "official" letter or document stating that you wish to remain in Taiwan for a legitimate purpose (usually to study Mandarin) in order to give the extension. Universities and some language centers now arrange work permits. In those cases, it is not necessary to study something in order to stay in the country, although you will probably want to study Mandarin if you wish to stay long-term.

Some "Chinese language centers" will make all the arrangements for a visa extension as part of their "tuition" for Mandarin classes that students do not attend (there are usually no actual classes; these "schools" only provide visa extensions). These centers operate through a legal loophole and it is best to check very carefully before using one to get an extension—your money is far better spent on real classes.

On a related note, you should try to keep your visa in perfect order and avoid overstaying—even by a couple of days—as those who overstay are sometimes labeled undesirable by immigration authorities and will not be allowed to return. This possibility is not revealed upon departure.

Police do, on very rare occasions, raid language centers during crackdowns on illegal workers, although these raids often consist of little more than a police officer or two paying a visit to the owner of the center, and possibly peeking into a couple of classrooms. The real focus is factories and construction sites. In Taiwan, as elsewhere, it is better to work legitimately than not to.

Regional politics (especially concerning the PRC) must be strictly avoided as a topic in conversation classes. Emotions run high in Taiwan when politics are involved (consider the fistfights at any meeting of the legislature), and English classes are hardly the place for such confrontations. One will still find that sections in encyclopedias and reference books concerning the PRC have been deleted or covered up.

While relations between Taiwan and the PRC have improved greatly in recent years, many aspects of both the international and local political arena may not be apparent to the average foreigner—and you could unintentionally cause offense.

The Peoples Republic of China

The PRC is certainly not the place for those teachers who are interested in making money, and it is arguably not the best place in the world for those who are interested in learning about traditional Chinese culture either. What you will find is a country very much in transition (yet again). The days of strictly segregated money (Chinese yuan RMB for Chinese and FECs, Foreign Exchange Certificates, for foreigners) and mandatorily segregated eating areas and two-tier menus in restaurants are nearly gone, but coal pollution, low pay, freezing-cold, one-room apartments with no hot water, bureaucracy, and noise are well entrenched.

Pushing all that aside, some of the most eager, although reticent, students in the region make the PRC an excellent choice for the truly dedicated teacher or one who wishes to gain experience quickly. Teaching in the PRC will present you with ample opportunity to test your abilities and patience in a very wide variety of classroom situations.

Most provincial capitals have a university, a college of science and technology, an arts institute, and a teachers' college, all of which are happy to have a "foreign expert" (requires a graduate degree) or "foreign teacher" (requires an undergraduate degree) as a member of their staff. The education division of the Chinese embassy is fairly strict about credentials if you apply by that route. Nevertheless, it is possible to apply directly to a school by letter or in person, and "the right attitude" can often take you further than credentials can. Many people have talked their way into jobs in China (a trend that began in 1275 with Marco Polo).

The PRC is an exception to the rule in that most letters of inquiry regarding job applications are actually answered, especially if you write to an individual rather than a department. Correspondence before arriving in person is recommended because it could save time spent untangling the red tape involved in getting a job. The person you correspond with may "guarantee'" or petition for your job application. Classes often *very* large are usually held six days a week, but your workload should be less than 40 hours. A Ph.D. holder typically earns about $350 dollars a month, while an undergraduate degree will bring in about $175. Perks often include housing, transportation, and food allowances. But do not set your expectations too high. The two-tier pricing system makes for a Spartan lifestyle (by Western standards) if you have no other source of income. Anticipate some bargaining at both ends. Bear in mind that, while some private companies are prospering, the central government is not. Even universities are trying to create their own profit centers. This could mean more money for teachers if a university is successful at generating income, or less if it must depend on a government payroll that is often months late. It is conceivable that one could work for an academic year and never get paid.

There is money to be made in the PRC—a lot of it. Some of the people making it are EFL teachers who spent years paying their dues (working for tiny salaries), and who became experts on the country in the process. They are now working as freelance advisors and consultants for large companies. In 1977, when Deng Xiaoping told the Chinese people to be "rich and glorious," his remark was taken at face value. Both Chinese entrepreneurs and well-informed foreigners are benefiting. Now more than ever, there is a contrast between northern and southern China. Even inexperienced teachers who work in the south may receive higher pay, and possibly pick up some, more lucrative extra teaching work with foreign companies.

As it does among the Chinese, *guanxi* (social connections), can improve a foreigner's lifestyle significantly. Working in the PRC can provide a crash course on that concept that is recommended to anyone who wishes to live long-term anywhere in Asia. The only way to truly understand the value of *guanxi* is to be put in a situation in which it is needed—and those situations abound in the PRC.

It is hard to give advice regarding what (and what not) to talk about in class because official attitudes tend to change with the wind. One might be required to use "We Love Labor" or "Different Lives in Different Societies," an interesting little passage about a Chinese worker and an American worker; the former works and is happy; the latter doesn't work and is unhappy. But many schools now use adaptations of popular international EFL textbooks. As a general guideline, avoid controversial topics, ask other teachers what they are presenting, and keep in mind the suggestions given throughout this book.

Again, the PRC is generally not a place for beginning teachers trying to maximize hours and make money, but the good and bad aspects of teaching there make it a good place to break into teaching EFL in Asia (as I did). Your experiences there will prove valuable in the future if you decide to continue teaching elsewhere—or to stay on and attempt to join those fortunate few who are becoming "rich and glorious."

Hong Kong

United Kingdom nationals have the best chance of finding work in Hong Kong. British accents are preferred. Other native English-speakers may have to look hard to find a job. Universities in Hong Kong generally offer programs of a high standard and with adequate pay.

The private language schools, on the other hand, are among the shoddiest in the region, and also the lowest paying. Good language centers are few, and those who depend on them as their only source of income will not be able to make ends meet. The majority of the good language centers recruit directly from the United Kingdom, although it is still possible to apply in person. At the other end of the spectrum, there is a language center in Kowloon to which you do not have to apply at all. Just walk in and write your name next to a class time on the board.

English is widely spoken in Hong Kong. Classes in many schools are conducted primarily in English, and language centers seem to mainly exist for the few instead of the majority.

At this time, I can only recommend teaching in Hong Kong to those who qualify for university positions or those who have other employment and wish to teach as a sideline.

South Korea

Korean schools offer a good salary, and universities, colleges, etc., have positions for native-English-speaking teachers. South Korea also has some of the strictest work permit regulations in the region. Work permits for language centers are arranged in advance through recruiting agencies, and the only realistic alternative for freelancers is to enter South Korea, apply for a job, and then leave the country (armed with the documents supplied by your new employer) and reapply for a work visa. In the long run, this method is better than using a recruiter because it results in higher salaries than those paid to recruited teachers. You will also be free to shop around and (maybe) work at more than one school. Some schools hire teachers who hold tourist visas on a temporary basis, but those planning long-term service should opt for the work visa. Regulations make working "under the table" in South Korea very complicated, and frequent visa runs are expensive. Those who wish to set up employment in advance could contact ELS International (a large language center that recruits in the United States for branches in many

East Asian countries and elsewhere. ELS International Inc., 5761 Buckingham Parkway, Culver City, CA 90230) or ask the South Korean embassy for details regarding current work permit regulations.

There are quite a few language centers in Seoul, and, as usual, they pay more than other schools. There is a preference in Korea for American accents and early morning classes (7 a.m.!) so late sleepers or those unaccustomed to such hours may have some problems. Dress is a bit formal—neckties for men and standard office attire for women.

Most teaching jobs at universities are set up in advance. Application in person is possible, but, again, you may need to leave the country in order to reapply for the proper visa.

Japan

Japanese schools offer the highest teacher salaries in the region. Even with the high cost of living, it is possible for teachers to put aside money and enjoy a good lifestyle. You will, of course, have to accept certain negative aspects of life in Japan, including cramped housing, and the high cost of living and entertainment. Another rough area is the unique love/hate relationship that Japan seems to have with the West. You will feel both admired and discriminated against, loved and hated, ignored and acknowledged, praised and scorned . . . often all at the same time. This is a fact of life throughout East Asia, but in Japan these mixed sentiments seem to be more obvious.

East/West cultural differences abound in Japan, but those who can accept them will find there the widest variety of teaching venues anywhere.

Universities, language centers, and other schools in Japan require at the minimum an undergraduate degree for teaching. Work visa regulations are similar to those in Korea. In the past, most freelance teachers worked "under the table" on tourist visas. Although regulations have gotten stricter, it is still possible to work on a tourist visa because there is a huge demand for Western teachers. It is best to apply in person, and as in Korea, it is possible that you will need to leave the county to reapply for a work visa. If you opt for a speculative job search, keep in mind that it takes several months to get settled in—and most schools pay by the month—so be sure to have sufficient funds to cover the interim between job hunting and getting paid.

Many schools in Japan rely on domestic and international agencies (ELS International, JET, ISES, YMCA, Berlitz, and many others). These agencies will arrange transportation, provide housing (often dormitory style), and a reasonable salary (around US $25,000). Nevertheless, teachers who apply in person earn more. The freedom of negotiating a job personally will appeal to those who plan to work long-term—while those interested in working for a year or so may be more attracted by the convenience of using an agency. Current information can be obtained from any Japanese embassy.

Accommodations are very expensive in Tokyo, and many teachers find it necessary to live in hostels. While new arrivals find some hostels in Tokyo to be good information sources, the transient atmosphere quickly grows tedious for most people, who then start the long search for reasonably priced accommodation in Tokyo, or move on to another city.

Private tutorials are very popular among Japanese, and teachers are often well paid. Fees of $60 an hour are not unheard of. While there are schools that specialize in sending teachers to private homes, most teachers are able to find enough of these opportunities on their own initiative. Those planning to work in Japan should study this book's suggestions on teaching privately (see page 11). Keep in mind that because private students come and go, it is difficult to depend on tutorials as your sole employment.

In addition to standard schools, the Japanese have come up with some interesting innovations of their own: telephone teaching, teaching on commuter trains, teaching by computer (via modem), and the infamous language lounge. Language lounges are primarily found in Japan although some have made their way to Taiwan and other parts of Northeast Asia. They are usually posh nightclub-like venues with a lounge area and private cubicles for one-by-one tutorials. Students come to the lounge and select a teacher for a 50-minute to one-hour study session. They can also stay in the lounge area and chat with other students and teachers.

Students have a wide variety of instructors to choose from—few of whom are even close to being qualified English teachers. These lounges are expensive, and the teachers' salaries depend on how often they are selected—a good conversationalist (often paid on a night-to-night basis) who can always come up with interesting discussion topics will quickly develop a regular clientele, while a quiet, intense type may have plenty of time—but no money—to ponder those weighty matters . . . alone.

English-teaching professionals condemn language lounges as being "linguistic prostitution of the worst kind carried out by impostors who are only interested in exploiting students and in making money." Possibly these moralists are among the fortunate who have never found themselves between jobs in Tokyo with the rent due the next week, and consequently can afford such opinions.

For many teachers, however, language lounges can provide both income and a venue to try new techniques and meet a wide variety of students individually, while looking for more traditional employment. For the student, they provide a very casual setting, and freedom to choose the teacher with whom they feel most comfortable. And they offer an opportunity to chat with native-English speakers from different cultural backgrounds—rare in Japanese society. No matter what the professionals think, many students who spend a year or so going to language lounges learn to do something that many other students who stick to traditional English study cannot: speak English.

The Japanese are generally very conscious of trends. In order to hold the interest of younger students (especially teenagers), it is important to keep classroom topics as up-to-date as possible. Also consider the age of your students when selecting class materials, as there is often little crossover of interests among age groups. A collection of teenagers would be happy to talk about skateboards and Kome Kome Club (a bizarre Japanese pop group) for hours, but adults would be lost. Adults might be able to explain the tea ceremony, while teenagers might think that this means getting together to carefully rip fashionable holes in T-shirts before a concert.

Other Parts of East Asia

In Malaysia, the Philippines, and Singapore, the opportunities for native English-speaking teachers are limited. English is widely spoken, there are many very capable local teachers, and most positions require related advanced degrees.

Schools in Brunei employee Western teachers, and salaries are high (per capita income in Brunei is about US$20,000). Apparently, the majority of hiring is done by recruiting agencies.

Some opportunities exist for experienced English teachers in Indochina. There are several government-run schools and a couple of private language centers in Vientiane, Laos, to which you must apply personally. There are also a few high-paying (U.S. wages, hardship posting), teaching jobs at various non-government organizations (NGOs) which obtain teachers through the organization's home office. Vietnam is considered by some to be the new frontier for teachers. Several private language centers have opened recently. There are many one-room language centers that offer English classes at a very low price. These are the result of supply and demand, and are usually run by local teachers supplementing their income. Teaching materials are few, but the quality of instruction can be high. Although many would be glad to employ Western teachers, most cannot afford to. Therefore, job hunts should focus on larger schools.

To look for work in either Laos or Vietnam, enter the country on a business visa that can be obtained from travel agencies in Bangkok that specialize in Indochina. Teachers are not permitted to work in either country with a tourist visa.

Currently, nearly all teaching jobs in Kampuchea (Cambodia) are with Western NGOs. These have strict standards and require related degrees. The few teaching jobs now available could disappear when the United Nations forces pull out—and certainly if the Khmer Rouge retake power. Potential teachers, like investors, should wait—perhaps a long time—for true stability.

As long as the policies of the junta in Myanmar (Burma) remain in force, teaching in that country will likely remain a difficult proposition. For now, job seekers should look elsewhere. Burma has recently flung open its doors to tourists, but they are still shut to foreign teachers. Much of the opposition in Burma is made up of student groups, and foreign teachers fan the flames.

And for those who are seeking more of a challenge, and one for which there is little advice . . . try North Korea.

Teaching EFL From the Start: Step by Step

Initially

Immerse yourself in TEFL. Study everything you can get your hands on (including TESL-based materials). Not all will be relevant, but it will at least provide a groundwork on which to develop your style.

Concentrate on classroom texts. Those listed in the bibliography of this book are commonly used in East Asia, and knowing something about them will prove valuable not only in the classroom, but also at job interviews. There are few veteran freelance teachers in East Asia who couldn't answer this one: "Where is Arno's Coffee Shop?" When you know the answer to that, you have done your homework well. (The answer can be found in a very popular ESL text.)

Decide where you want to focus your job hunt and find out everything you can about it. Large libraries may have telephone books (the best source of information on language centers) from large Asian cities. General books and magazines on working abroad will also have some information. If you focus on a country, instead of a particular city, maps in guidebooks will show the larger cities (most have language centers).

Determine a few alternatives. If you go to Japan and don't like it, Korea and Taiwan are nearby.

If you decide to use a recruiter, shop around to find the one that best suits your needs. The one you choose will take care of everything from there (not very adventurous, huh?) and you can concentrate on researching the people and the country you intend to teach in.

If you take the freelance route (bravo!), get all your documents (degrees, transcripts, certificates) together and apply for the longest-term visa you can get. Embassies in the West are often more generous about issuing long visas than those in East Asia. If you don't have a degree, consider taking a TESL/TEFL certificate program in the West, or far better, in East Asia.

You will need money. Three thousand dollars can finance a six-month job hunt in Southeast Asia; about half that in Northeast Asia. It is easier to maximize hours in Northeast Asia, reducing the period of negative cash flow. Finding a job may only take a few days, but you will need money until you have enough hours. The most important factor in finding a job quickly is to learn when terms start. Different schools start terms at different times, but if you arrive the day after a term has begun at a language center, there might be a six weeks' wait for new work. If you are planning to wait a few months before leaving, consider sending several "letters of introduction" to language centers in your target area explaining when you will be there, and that you would like an interview. Ask them for a schedule of term dates, and inquire about local language classes. Whether or not you are actually interested, potential customers have a better chance of getting a reply than potential teachers. Most letters will probably not be answered, but they do let people know that you are coming. Any information is valuable. Even if you only get a brochure explaining a local language course, it will tell you something about the school.

Departing

Plan for your trip as if you were taking a long vacation. Don't burn any bridges, but don't leave any loose ends either. You might want to put some things you would like to have once you get settled (a barrel of jalapeño peppers?) in a carton to be shipped by a friend. Travel light and *don't use a backpack*. The image you project should be up-market even if your budget isn't. Look good when you travel. You never know what will happen.

When I first arrived in Taiwan, I wanted to avoid Taipei, so I called a language school in Taichung from the airport. The director said they needed teachers, and I asked if he could recommend a hotel. He told me to come directly to the school, so I got on a bus to Taichung, and arrived at the language center with all my gear. I ended up sleeping in a class-room for two weeks until the new term started. Had I been carrying a backpack and dressed like a tourist, I would not have gotten that job, at which I worked intermittently for six years.

Arriving

Get right on it. Find a place to stay, a telephone, and a phone book. The phone book might not be in English, but the logos of the language centers are. The large language centers listed in this book are also a good place to start.

Advertisements for teachers can also be found in the classified sections of English language newspapers. Bulletin boards at the local United States Information Service (USIS), British Council, and university English departments frequently have signs posted requesting teachers. Get on the phone, and find out a few things about each school. Ask about the classes they offer, where they are located, when the term starts, and if they need teachers. Don't apply on the phone. Just ask a few questions, and see what they say. Telephoning in East Asia can be very frustrating, so do not expect conclusive results. At this point, you are only trying to evaluate the job market.

After locating some potential employers, continue your job market evaluation in person. Visit some language centers and the English departments at a couple of universities. Be prepared to apply, but your main goal should be information. It should only take a few days to evaluate a city this way. If job prospects are promising, stay on. If they aren't, move on to the next city.

If you decide to stay, look for a short-lease (monthly) furnished apartment in a university area. The tourist areas to which Westerners tend to gravitate are too expensive and insular. Short-lease apartments are often a little more expensive than regular unfurnished ones, but you don't want to start buying furniture while you are still getting organized. A telephone where you can be reached is essential. Also, get some name cards printed up (a cheap, ten-minute job if the shop has a computer with a font program and a laser printer). Have them printed on one side in English and the other in the local language. Once you are teaching a few hours, concentrate on the job, but do not stop looking for additional work.

Once you have enough hours, and everything is beginning to shape up, start looking for more comfortable housing. Also consider making a few investments. As soon as I know that I am going to stay somewhere, I buy a motorcycle. Motorcycles are the main form of transportation in East Asia, and although driving one is probably one of the most dangerous activities that one could participate in (barring juggling hand grenades), the freedom they offer is worth the hospital bills (I am, unfortunately, quite familiar with the orthopedic wards of several East Asian hospitals). The "cheap used car" does not exist in East Asia (very high import duties), so for most people, it's a motorcycle or the bus. New motorcycles start at around $1,000, and used ones can be had for much less, except in Japan where there is no market for used anything. A refrigerator, a TV/VCR, a dog, and about a thousand other things rate above furniture on my list of priorities—better to follow your own priorities. If you bring consumer electronics from home, remember that getting them serviced might be impossible in East Asia—it's better to buy locally.

Finally

No matter what country you choose to work in, what venue you decide to teach in, or what materials you use in class, at the center of things is the successful interaction between teacher and student. The following sections: The Teacher, The Student, and The Class can help start you off in the right direction.

Two

The Teacher

Qualifications (or the Lack Thereof)
Can Anyone Really Teach English?

EFL can differ from other fields in that one can have few qualifications, no related experience, and still do a great job.

It is unlikely that a waiter who tired of his work would walk into a rocket factory on a whim and declare, "I am an aerospace engineer." Yet, that same waiter might use his last paycheck on a plane ticket to East Asia, walk into a language school or a university and say, "I am an English teacher." There is even a fair chance he would be hired.

The goal of an EFL teacher is to teach students to do something that anyone who is able to read this book can do: communicate in English. The knowledge required for the job is already there. It will probably need some refining—no more than can be had from a few evenings with a good text on English usage—and it may take anywhere from a few weeks to a few years to work out how to best apply it in the classroom. Nonetheless, native-English-speakers have had experience in this field since birth, and little stands in the way of those who wish to make a living at it.

This is not to say that anyone can work anywhere. Requirements for teaching positions can run from a compulsory masters degree in applied linguistics to a polite request to wear a clean shirt. The type of school can range from a top-notch university to a small room in the back of a motorcycle repair shop.

The majority of teaching venues in East Asia do require a university degree of some kind. Most universities require a related degree (English, TEFL, or other humanities-based) while full-time positions at universities usually require specific advanced degrees (English, TEFL, Applied Linguistics, etc.). But at some schools an undergraduate degree in accounting could land one the position of English department head. It largely depends on supply and demand.

An alternative for those who do not have a degree is a certificate from one of the TEFL training centers located worldwide. These programs take about one month of full-time study or three months of part-time study to complete. The certificates awarded are accepted by many language centers, and even a few universities, in place of a university degree. Enrollment in these programs is open to anyone. Some language centers pay new teachers' tuition fees to these programs. Approval by TESOL (Teachers of English to Speakers of Other Languages) is a widely recognized sign of credibility. Be sure that a program has been formally approved before enrolling.

Perhaps the most respected TEFL certification program is the RSA (Royal Society of the Arts) course. The RSA course consists of 100 hours of study, and the certificate earned is required for teaching positions at British Council language centers in Asia and elsewhere. Many other language centers accept the RSA certificate, and some sponsor RSA courses. One such sponsor is ECC (THAILAND) which offers the RSA/CTEFLA (Cambridge Certificate of Teaching English as a Foreign Language to Adults) course twice a year in Bangkok. Write ECC [Thailand] 430/17-24 Chula Soi 64, Siam Square, Patumwan, Bangkok 10330, Thailand. After two years of teaching, teachers who hold an RSA certificate are eligible for an RSA diploma which is accepted at language centers and universities worldwide. Those interested in the RSA can contact RSA, International Teachers Training Institute, International House, 106 Piccadilly, London WlV 9FL, for more information.

Professionalism in the Classroom

One very important aspect of teaching EFL is professionalism in the classroom. This is true in any educational area, but the amount of unprofessionalism Asians have been subjected to makes it all the more important there. East Asia was—and may still be—the world capital of EFL teachers who have no idea what method they should use. While TEFL credentials may have little bearing on whether or not you can teach, it is essential to have some idea of what to do, an above-average grasp of the English language, and a sincere desire help your students.

Students are becoming more aware of how to tell a legitimate teacher from an impostor, and some language centers and student-oriented publications in East Asia are making a good effort to help people tell the difference. For example, *The Nation Junior,* a biweekly magazine for EFL students published by *The Nation,* one of Thailand's leading English-language newspapers, recently ran a cover story entitled "Kao Sarn Road Teachers—and how to avoid them." Kao Sarn Road, an area in Bangkok in which most of the city's cheap guest houses are now located, has become the central meeting place for the down-and-out, both Thai and Western. This part of town is looked down upon by most Thais and is avoided by most well-informed visitors. Most of the travel horror stories told by tourists who have been cheated in various scams originate from this area—and so do some of the worst "EFL teachers" on the face of the earth.

The magazine's cover photo showed a group of immaculately dressed Thai students (in all honesty, I should mention that the group in the photo was somewhat better dressed than any class I have ever seen) listening to a tattooed, disheveled, Western teacher who was standing at the whiteboard trying to write his name while listening to a Walkman and smoking a cigarette, his hairy navel peeking out from the bottom of his T-shirt.

The article said that many language teachers lack training in the field and are actually "instructors" (read: impostors) and not qualified teachers. There were also quotes from several disenchanted students along the lines of "We had six different teachers in a four-week term." "All my teacher did was talk about Guns 'n' Roses and tell us about India." "I asked my teacher how to spell 'special' —he wrote S-P-E-C-A-L on the board." "On the first day of class my teacher asked me out on a date."

I have heard complaints like these before (not usually about me), and they only reveal the tip of the iceberg. Asian students are becoming wary about who they will learn from, and owners of language schools realize that they have to present a quality product or shut their doors. As a result, the demand for competent teachers is increasing.

Successfully teaching East Asian students involves both having the right attitude and acquiring a deep understanding of the learning environment in which they feel most at ease. There are as many facets to understanding the right attitude and gaining insight into students' needs and motivations as there are ways of using the knowledge one gains.

The key to pleasing students is professionalism. This means dressing the part that the host society deems appropriate for the position, being well-versed in most aspects of the language, preparing relevant material, starting and stopping class on time, keeping social life separate from the classroom, remaining neutral in opinions, and genuinely caring about helping students.

Those with a Western education are familiar with the informal methods common among Western teachers. Most Asian students are not. Asians tend to think of all teachers as being on a higher level of existence. The informality that we are comfortable with is hard to attain in an Asian classroom, and just getting students to call us by our names, and not "teacher," or to think of us on equal terms, is a challenge for anyone.

Legitimate Western English teachers can be mistaken for impostors simply by a few blunders in dress and manner. Things like sitting on desks, dating students, and using bizarre methodology—even with good intentions—often have a negative effect. This is not to say that creativity (or any of the above) is prohibited: it is just far better to learn the limits before attempting to stretch them.

Successful teachers also avoid playing the rebel in societies in which rebels are looked down upon—especially in those societies in which the teacher is expected to be the "good girl/boy" at all times. It is rather unrealistic to think that it would be possible to change the social and moral values of an entire society during a six-week language course—in between explaining how to use a past participle and how to order a cup of coffee with cream but no sugar.

Even gestures and comments that are considered harmless by most Westerners can be considered unprofessional, inappropriate, or even offensive in some societies.

In *Forum*, a journal for English teachers, Gao Yihong, a teacher at Beijing University, wrote that she had participated in a training workshop in which a visiting language-teaching "specialist" had introduced some new techniques that (he said) had proven to be very successful in language classes in the United States. Techniques mentioned included activities involving finger snapping, touching students, pretending to cry, kissing and hugging students, and kneeling and begging students to come to the front of the class.

None of the actions above are part of the body-language repertoire of the average Chinese teacher, and Ms. Gao noted that the finger-snapping took a great deal of practice—and sore fingers—to master. She also mentioned that finger snapping (and pointing) is an action more associated with young hooligans than with nice young English teachers.

Ms. Gao actually tried these techniques out on her students and issued a questionnaire for them to fill out after the class: 54 percent of her 32 students responded positively and 41.6 percent responded negatively to the finger snapping and pointing activity (I don't know what she did with the other 7.4 percent). Of the students who didn't like the activity, half said it showed disrespect for them and the other half said it made them nervous; 71 percent didn't like the hugging and kissing; 12.5 percent thought it was interesting (16.5 percent missing here).

In a discussion after the activity, one student "shouted" that the teacher's odd gestures could have run the students out of the classroom. A second said, "Since we are Chinese and are now in China, we should behave in the Chinese way." Another commented that "the kissing shows what a loving teacher we have, but the kneeling makes her lose the respect of her students."

It is important to consider that the teacher who tried these activities was female and Chinese. Had it been a male Westerner doing the hugging and kissing, the students would have definitely run out of the classroom—and quite likely straight to the nearest police officer. The English department at Beijing University was probably shanghaied. The language training specialist obviously was not a specialist at training Chinese or he would have adapted his methods to be more culturally appropriate.

Professionalism in the classroom depends on the expectations of a society as a whole, and our own ideas in this regard are not always right on the mark.

A good teacher with a professional manner can do a great job in the worst school. With natural talent—or a bit of experience—that same teacher can also ply his or her trade almost anywhere he or she chooses.

What Makes a Good Teacher?

If credentials do not always make a good teacher, then what does? The following list, compiled from comments made by students during classes on this topic, will give some insight:

A good EFL teacher:

explains things	makes us laugh
doesn't embarrass us	knows about our lives
doesn't talk too much	dresses politely
knows a lot of games	speaks clearly
starts and stops on time	doesn't give homework
gives homework	treats us like people
makes grammar simple	is educated
is a good example	is informal
is good at acting	uses body language
teaches us natural English	is lively
doesn't always use the book	is experienced
asks everybody questions	talks at our level

gets us to do what we need to do without pushing

And the bad teacher?

is strict	has a bad temper
is not prepared	only reads the book
looks dead	wears dirty clothes
is too busy for us	makes things difficult
has a blank face	makes many mistakes

only talks to the girls (male teacher)

Other comments are more personal: "A good teacher is rich and takes us to dinner every night"; "A good teacher teaches us dirty words so we can understand movies," and (one of my favorites) "A bad teacher has Hong Kong Foot" ("Hong Kong Foot" is a term used to describe foot odor in several Asian languages; it is beyond the scope of this text to do more than bring this to the reader's attention).

One can infer from these student comments that there is a bit more to teaching than just walking into a room and talking. There is also more to teaching a language than simply knowing how to speak it.

Knowledge of how to apply what you know about English to teaching comes from either study or on-the-job training. Study usually takes the form of TESL/EFL courses or degree programs, and on-the-job training is gained from simply getting in there and doing it. Many schools offer some form of teacher training or another—the value of which depends on the teaching experience of the trainer.

Training and Results

Those whose training comes from TEFL courses tend to have rather high expectations—at first anyway—regarding the amount of learning that actually happens in an EFL class. Many of their techniques are not suitable for East Asian students. Theory does not often work out as well in practice as it does on a linguistic theorist's word processor. Many graduates of TEFL programs need to be retrained if they plan to teach long-term in East Asia, as they often seem somewhat overwhelming in the eyes of their students and more practical colleagues.

Those who learn on the job only know what they have seen in the classroom. These teachers are more forgiving with their students, and often too easily satisfied. Teachers who have only learned on the job often leave out the fundamental aspects of the topics and structures that they teach. There are, of course, positive aspects to both types of training. TEFL graduates are well versed in the fundamentals of the language. They can give their students a solid base on which to improve their abilities.

In the classrooms of teachers who have been trained on the job, real communication takes place—the goal of any English class. Nevertheless, the students may well leave at the end of the class period with no idea of how that communication took place or how to use any of the language in a situation outside the classroom. The discerning teacher will adopt the best of both types of training in a manner relevant to each specific group of students.

The Right Attitude

New EFL teachers in East Asia have diverse attitudes toward their students, while more experienced teachers seem to differ more in approach than viewpoint about Asians. This indicates that there is a generally correct attitude, the basis of which is the ability to see and relate to students as they are, and not just as one thinks they should be—while methodology is more a matter of personal choice. Those with the wrong attitude don't last long in the profession. Asian students don't habitually run to the director whenever something disagreeable happens in class (although complaints are encouraged), but a teacher's attitude can be accurately judged by class attendance. If there is a sharp drop-off early in the term, something is definitely wrong. Some schools try to screen out incompatible teachers early in the application process with a questions on the application form such as, "In your opinion, what is the primary role of an EFL teacher?" Here are some answers given by applicants at a language center in Taiwan:

> "I think that the main role of an EFL teacher is to teach students to speak the English language correctly. Errors are embarrass- ing for the speaker and hard on the ears of the listener. Most errors stem from laziness on the part of the student, and I have developed various methods which proved effective in the remedial English classes I taught in the United States."

> "The purpose of an EFL teacher is to act as a guide through the complex maze that we call English grammar. Students of English should first learn the basics of grammar before moving on to speaking and conversation."

> "People in this country are wrong about the way they are teaching students. My extensive experience (25 years) teaching in the United States and Europe has shown that in order to speak English fluently the student must learn to speak out about his or her opinions on topics that are of major concern in the world today. Besides teaching English, a teacher should help students along the road to international understanding by presenting topics that will broaden their horizons and general outlook about the world situation."

> "Learning English should be fun. It is cruel to shove a bunch of incomprehensible grammar down the throats of students when that is done to them already throughout high school. I think that students can learn a great deal from talks about my own experi- ences in their country (and abroad) and benefit from my suggestions on how to improve it."

I didn't hire any of them, and did not even grant an interview. They all seemed confident about what they wrote, but in my opinion, they all missed the mark. They didn't see their students (or themselves) clearly or realistically enough to be good teachers. The applicant who wrote the following did get hired:

> "I think that the primary goal of an EFL teacher would be to act as an example of a native speaker and to provide materials to help elicit natural conversation from students without the teacher taking the dominating role common in other forms of teaching. Of course she should teach, but it should be done in a way that allows the majority of the input to be given by students."

This teacher had the right attitude. She had little training in teaching; however, her opinions were based on her own experiences in studying a foreign language. Those who have spent time taking language classes often have the best ideas about what does and does not work. Since the language she had studied was Japanese, she also had a good idea about what is and is not acceptable in an East Asian classroom. After being hired, she completed a few sessions of teacher training, and went on to become an excellent teacher who received superb in-class evaluations. She eventually became a teacher-trainer herself.

In-class evaluations are another way language centers keep tabs on attitude and teaching ability. Some evaluations are given by teacher trainers or curriculum directors. Other schools supply students with evaluation forms to fill out. Some teachers even make up their own evaluation sheet and use the results to monitor themselves in the hopes of catching bad habits and improving on good ones. The following evaluation is used by the director and teacher trainer for in-class observations at AUA Language Center in Chiang Mai, Thailand:

1. Classroom Arrangement
Does the seating arrangement serve the purpose of instruction? Does seating permit the class to hear the teacher and other students? Is the seating arrangement suitable for classroom interaction? Is the cassette player centrally located so that it can be heard clearly?

2. Administration

Does the teacher properly use class cards and take accurate attendance? Does the teacher start and stop class on time?

3. Preparation and Knowledge of Content

Does the teacher seem well prepared and knowledgeable about the content, functions, structure and vocabulary, story line, cultural points of the material being taught? Does the teacher follow the recommended structural sequences and techniques? Does the teacher provide "real" situations that give students opportunities to use the items studied in their books in a communicative way? Does the teacher personalize the material in the text by asking about students' opinions and experiences? Does the teacher use training aids such as posters, cards, realia, pictures, worksheets, cassettes, blackboard or whiteboard, and games?

4. Classroom Management

Does the teacher control the class, i.e. involving the students in an activity where everyone's attention is focused? Does the teacher take care that both males/females, bright/average/below-average, quick/reflective, students are questioned and get to answer? Does the teacher distribute questions evenly by calling on everyone? Does the teacher get too close to students in individual work with the result that the rest of the class cannot hear the repetition and correction? Does the teacher cue students who are slow or reluctant to answer? Does the teacher use techniques to gain attention and motivate the students at the beginning of the lesson?

5. Instruction

Does the teacher provide clear and effective instructions? Does the teacher provide a good model? (Speaking clearly and at a natural rate following marked intonation and stress?) Does the teacher use Thai just for expediency and not as a procedure? Does the teacher use extra-linguistic cues (gesture, dramatization?) Does the teacher use simple, concise language when explaining difficult vocabulary and concepts? Does the teacher take up class time with long explanations, expositions, or personal comments?

6. Classroom Interaction

Does the teacher seek opportunities for the students to do most of the talking? Is there student-to-student as well as student-to-teacher interaction? Does the teacher involve the students in pair- work, group-work, whole class, interaction? Does the teacher vary the pairs/groups (old/young, male/female), and separate friends from each other?

7. Review, Monitoring, and Correction Techniques

Does the teacher monitor student speech and correct student responses sufficiently and at the appropriate time? Are error corrections being done in non-intrusive ways? Does the teacher review the previous lesson at the beginning of the class? Does the teacher monitor what students write in their textbooks?

8. Classroom Manner and Rapport

Is the tempo of class work lively? Are the students interested, attentive, and cooperative? Does the teacher present the material in a non-perfunctory manner? Does the teacher call students by name? Does the teacher seem familiar with the personal background of some of the students (work, study)? Does the teacher stand most of the time? Does the teacher use disciplinary action that is appropriate and in accordance with cultural norms?

9. Personal Attributes

Is the teacher neat and well dressed? Is the teacher alert and confident? Does the teacher have a patronizing or overcritical attitude? Does the teacher have any undesirable or distracting mannerisms? Does the teacher remain in control of emotions by not showing anger or frustration? Does the teacher display awareness of cultural norms specific to Thailand?

Some new teachers are surprised at how detailed that evaluation is (it is the most thorough I have ever seen). It would seem impossible to measure up to such standards, even if performance is assessed over several class periods. Nevertheless, most experienced EFL teachers are able to meet most of these criteria in every class, automatically. New teachers should attempt to do the same.

The other kind of evaluation is the teacher-generated version given to students as a means of self-assessment. This type of evaluation is of limited value in East Asia, because of a general aversion to public criticism. To be criticized or to criticize others publicly causes a loss of face all around. Negative opinions are usually expressed privately, among friends. Nevertheless, if worded properly, evaluations can be useful to the teacher as well as a viable way for students to air their opinions indirectly. It is essential that these evaluations remain anonymous. Most teachers who use them find that they are answered more fully if written in the students' native language. A teacher-generated evaluation might use some of the following questions:

About the Class Content:
Do I speak clearly? Do I plan well and present interesting material? Are my questions easy to answer? Do I use the board appropriately? Do I use teaching aids enough?

About the Book:
Do you think the book is interesting? Do you think it is clear? Do you think it is well laid-out? Do you think it is suitable for your level? Do you think it is suitable for your age group? Does it present English in situations that can be used in everyday life?

About the Teacher:
Do you think I enjoy teaching students of your age and level? Do I seem relaxed? Do you think I have a thorough knowledge of English? Am I experienced? Am I moody or sarcastic? Do you think that you are making progress in my class?

About Teacher-Student Interaction:
Have I ever embarrassed you in front of the rest of the class? Do I give you time to think about your answer before calling on you? Do I try to help you? Do I praise you at appropriate times?

About Teacher-Class Interaction:
Do I distribute questions evenly among the students? Do I give everyone an equal chance to talk? Do I have a favorite student?

Do you think your class likes me? Am I patient with slow learners? Am I too strict? Am I too easygoing?

This type of evaluation generally gives the students a choice among "yes," "no," or "sometimes" for each question, with a space left at the bottom for additional comments. You may be surprised at how candid students can actually be with this type of anonymous questionnaire in both their positive and negative input. Although no one can be expected to please all students at all times, the answers on all types of evaluations can be an accurate gauge of whether or not you are on the right track when it comes to attitude and manner in the classroom. They can also inform you of whether it is time to try some new techniques or hold on to some that you were not sure about. A good teacher trainer will be able to interpret the answers found on an evaluation and provide suggestions on how to improve performance in any trouble areas.

Teacher Training or Learn as You Go?

If you are not sure what actually happens in an EFL classroom, or if you have limited experience, you might wonder about teacher training. Some Western programs of the type that offer a certificate after a short course could shed some light on the basic goals of teaching EFL, although many people believe that their value—at least when it comes to teaching Asian students—is questionable, as most of the course content is geared toward teaching Europeans or ESL.

Certificate Programs

The following two American programs offer short courses, and a certificate from either is accepted by some language centers in place of a diploma.

St. Giles Educational Trust
2280 Powell Street
San Francisco, CA 94133

Transworld Teachers
683 Sutter
San Francisco, CA 94102

There is no solid evidence to prove that those who graduate from certificate programs are better prepared to teach than those who do not, and personal observation often indicates the reverse. It is impossible for any training program to provide what an individual needs in order to be a successful EFL teacher. That will only come with experience. Certificate programs in Asia, however, may well be worth the time and money for novice teachers, because these programs focus on more relevant teaching techniques. They are also less expensive than courses in the West. These programs require active participation and often grade potential teachers on actual classroom teaching. The students taught during training courses in Asia are typical East Asian EFL students (upper-income overachievers) while those taught in the West are often lower-income immigrants of different backgrounds and nationalities. (Asian students who go to the United States solely to study English usually attend up-market ESL programs like those offered by Georgetown University, or the University of Wisconsin-Steven's Point. These programs employ experienced teachers). The approaches used when teaching students from different ethnic and economic backgrounds should also be different.

Most in-house training programs clarify how the school itself operates and the prescribed way to use the textbook. Most language centers try to loosely orchestrate the use of textbooks so that the promised amount of material will be covered during a term and students will be prepared to move to the next level. A teacher trainer may explain step-by-step how the book is used, or may just say something like "we try to cover about two pages a day." Few schools actually sit you down and start throwing theories in your face, and rarely do language centers require active involvement in their training. You will probably not be asked to demonstrate what you learned before being allowed to teach a class. Most trainers will simply explain what should be done and when. A good trainer will also include information about the students themselves. "I think that might be a quiet group, you might want to try one of these warm-up activities to get them going," or "Most of those students are office workers. They are coming here after work, so try to use interactive activities and don't lecture, or they will fall asleep on you." Most schools will also provide a "teacher's guide" of sorts that may come in handy.

You will probably also be asked to observe several classes. This is the best type of training there is. You will see how an experienced teacher handles a class and how that teacher deals with slow students, shy students, and various other situations that outside training cannot prepare you for. You will also be able to pick up tips regarding technique and the use of the textbook. A good trainer will arrange situations in which the teacher observing the class can see how various types of materials are used in that school with those students. Ideally, a question-and-answer session will be arranged after the class so that the new teacher can put what was observed into perspective and any unclear areas can be explained. Even if the school offers no teacher training, a new teacher should ask to sit in on a class or two (or several). The insight gained from those few classes is likely to be far more comprehensive and practical than the methodology and theory taught elsewhere.

Most of your technique will be learned on the job from trial and error. Even the most experienced teachers find themselves walking out of the classroom at the end of an occasional class-period saying, "That was the worst class I have ever taught." Nevertheless, teacher training is a valuable way to reduce the number of those days, and it helps get you started on the right track.

Adaptation: Go Roman?

Once a teacher starts feeling comfortable with technique, cultural differences might overshadow otherwise effective teaching. Even a well-planned class can fail if the teacher does something that the students find embarrassing or that makes them uncomfortable. Many of the activities tried by the above-mentioned teacher in Beijing simply do not fit into the cultural norms of present-day Chinese society. But the key element in her experimentation is that she is Chinese. She is, arguably, in a position to try new things that the students may consider to be odd, and she can still hold onto her job—and the respect of her students. The Western teacher does not always fare so well. Students' reactions to the unusual can range from simple and often well disguised embarrassment to dropping the course, depending on how much of a faux pas the teacher is guilty of and the general attitude of the students.

A simple way to avoid problems might be to "go Roman," and try to do everything the way locals would. But, one can't realistically "go Roman" if the Romans won't allow it. The adage is not relevant in Asia, as locals often expect foreigners to operate under completely different sets of rules. A more appropriate saying, at the beginning, would be, "When in Rome, act like a guest of the Romans." Later, "When in Rome, don't step on the Romans' toes" is the maxim. This allows us to watch and learn the way things are done. Finally, we can operate within the local cultural framework, maintain our own cultural identities, and be creative in class (or elsewhere) without causing offense. This is the essence of active adaptation.

It can be difficult for a Westerner to actively adapt to an East Asian society. Lifestyles can appear so different that some find it easier to criticize than to accept. A psychological island based on "us" and "them" is built. The way "we" do everything is right; the way "they" do anything is wrong. One would certainly want to avoid the folly of the "Ugly American" or the "Obnoxious Brit." "Why can't anybody in this country drive?" "Why can't anyone keep a promise?" "Doesn't anyone in this country ever do anything besides watch TV?" I have even seen this kind of questioning in the classroom. Average students of English would have nothing to compare themselves to and would be unable to answer these kinds of questions even if they wanted to. Teachers ask such questions because they are made comfortable by students who have been brought up to be good hosts. The sense of ease they create leads the Westerner to raise topics that are bound to make students feel uneasy.

It is common to make the mistake of unfavorably comparing a host country with one's own. The text in one of my university courses contained the seemingly innocuous question, "Can you name some famous Thai scientists." My students and I couldn't come up with any— not on the same level as those mentioned in the text (Galileo, Kepler, Darwin, Einstein, etc.). The writer of that text must not have known that any discussion based on such questions would be humiliating to the students. Why not just, "Can you name some scientists?"

If questions that might illuminate the shortcomings of a particular country, region, or area must brought up, it is far better for the teacher to remain neutral by introducing the topic indirectly. If you want to know what people think about TV, ask. But don't compare judgmentally. Keep your discussion neutral. In a class in Beijing, if I wanted to talk about driving, for example, I would say, "A Chinese friend from here said that people in Shanghai don't drive as well as people in Beijing. Is that true? It is? Why do you say that? Do many people here think that?" and so on. Raising the topic in this manner can still cause problems (depending on how many students in the class are from Shanghai). Nevertheless, the problems are likely to be among the students and not between them and the teacher. This could make for a lively class discussion, or the students may drop the topic on their own. In any case, the teacher remains neutral and class will be aware of it.

Accepting local concepts of proper dress is a big step toward adaptation. In general, Asians place a high value on appearance, and EFL teachers are expected to dress the part of their role in society. A typical misconception regarding clothing is the idea that dressing like a local farmer somehow indicates that the wearer has some kind of insight into the local culture. This notion is more common among tourists than teachers, but it has been an issue at every school at which I have worked. Baggy cotton pants, tank-tops, sandals, shorts, mock-ethnic "local" attire and other "budget traveler" apparel have no place in the classroom—or anywhere else besides the beach, for that matter. This does not mean that EFL teachers all run around wearing business suits; just clean, conservative casual clothes.

Just as some find it convenient to reject a culture, there is also a tendency to "over-adapt." "You're in ASIA! How can you sit there eating PIZZA and listening to THE CLASH in ASIA? You should be eating FRIED RICE and listening to RAVI SHANKAR and KITTARO." The culturally aware teacher will try to find a midpoint and keep to it.

While working as a teacher trainer in Taiwan, I was once presented, by group of students from an upper-level class, with a photocopy of one teacher's interpretation of the *I Ching*, which he had used in class. The students had hardly heard of it, and they wanted to know what relevance such an obscure work could possibly have to learning English.

Agreeing that the material was unsuitable, I arranged a conference with the teacher. When I brought up the complaint made by his students, he said that he thought that the Chinese were forgetting their cultural roots and that he was trying to help them remember. I suggested that the movie section of the newspaper would be a far more useful and interesting way to localize the content of the lesson than to try to use literature familiar only to students involved in specialized study. He didn't realize that the *I Ching* was far more popular with his Western friends than it was with Chinese high-school students.

On another occasion, while making unannounced observations of classes in Thailand (I was involved in training at that school, but not hiring), I came across a group of students sitting on the floor being led by a teacher in what could have only been a form of meditation. The teacher was sitting in a lotus position chanting "OMMMMMMMMMMMM," and the students turned to me with pleading looks on their faces.

Once again, a conference was in order. The teacher suggested that the students needed to relax and clear their minds before class. I was curious how a group of students—most of whom were wearing office attire—could relax while sitting on a dirty floor looking at an American sitting in a very unattractive position chanting an incomprehensible mantra when they were supposed to be learning about how to take a message on the telephone.

I suggested further that they might find that situation confusing.

"They know about meditation," she said.

"They know not to do it in English class," I mentioned.

"You don't understand."

"I understand they were sitting on the floor."

"Thais like to sit on the floor!" She was becoming indignant.

"Thais like to sit on a clean floor."

"You still don't understand."

"I don't need to understand. These people spend a lot more time watching TV and going shopping than they do trying to become one with the universe."

"That's the problem."

"That's not the problem. The problem is that these people came here to learn how to speak English so they can talk to Ted the Fabric Buyer from Texas and make a nice commission so they can buy a VCR, and instead they have to listen to the uninformed ravings of a Sears version of Mahatma Gandhi! (Are you a real Gandhi or a Sears Gandhi?)" I was on a roll.

"You are part of the problem," she suggested.

"I think you would be far more comfortable handing out pamphlets from inside a cage at an American airport than you are attempting to teach here."

"You are promoting the death of a culture."

"At least this culture will die with clean trouser bottoms, sitting at a desk, knowing how to take a message on the telephone in English."

With that, she walked out the door never to be seen again. My side of the argument is probably more eloquent in the retelling than it was originally, but this was the gist of our discussion.

The point of the two examples is that some teachers do have unusual notions about modern Asian society. They expect the average student of English to be well informed in the often obscure facets of their cultures that some Westerners find intriguing. But if such students did happen to be interested in Chinese philosophy or meditation, they would take specialized courses in it, and those courses would be in their own language, taught by recognized experts.

One key to adaptation to any society is to become familiar with what is currently popular in that society. Pop music provides more clues than pop psychology; more people relax in front of the TV than in a lotus position; movies are more popular than traditional theater; the well-known tells more about the culture than the obscure. That is the way it is, whether we like it or not. It is not the job of the EFL teacher to attempt to change it. Local cultural topics can be introduced by the students, probably prompted by the teacher:

"There is a holiday tomorrow, isn't there?"
"What do people do during this holiday?"
"Isn't there a story behind this holiday?"

The teacher can then provide details that the students leave out or have trouble vocalizing. After several years of teaching, many teachers become more familiar with local holidays and other customs than most students are, simply because they have been discussed so many times in previous years with such a wide variety of students from different local backgrounds.

A working knowledge of the local entertainment industry (movies, actors and actresses, music groups and singers, song names and lyrics, TV shows) can help a foreigner adapt to a culture by providing insight into what people are actually seeing and doing in everyday life. Few Western teachers know more than the basics of these topics and often consider them unimportant. Students are amazed when they have a teacher who is well informed. Knowing the story line of a popular soap opera is unconditionally guaranteed to be more useful in class than the ability to chant in Urdu while standing on your head. Adaptation to the classroom in Asia is an objective experience that is best approached with an open mind and a minimum of preconceptions.

Preconceptions and Stereotypes

The preconceptions held by Westerners about Asians and vice-versa are the root of many problems that arise in the EFL classroom. Some Westerners tend to define Asians according to stereotypes based on Asian characters with whom they have been made familiar by the media. These characters are, of course, no better an example of the personalities found in Asia than Rambo is an example of the typical American male. You would be hard pressed to find a 1990s' version of David Carridine's *Grasshopper* sitting among your EFL students. The relentless flood of media images throughout our lives has given us all false impression of Asia and Asians (and Asians of Westerners as well as of each other). To excite its audience, the media has focused on the ritualistic Asia and highlighted the exotic aspects of Asia, while intentionally ignoring the facets of life, increasingly numerous today, that are similar to ours. To prove this, you need only close your eyes and think of an Asian country that you have never visited. Unless you are very well informed, images out of tourist brochures are sure to appear before images of modern shopping centers and BMW dealerships. (When I think of Sri Lanka, a Duran Duran video, of all things, dominates my mental images. I am probably not alone in that).

The ritualistic Asia is truly vivid. The more vivid the ritual, the less comprehensible it is to the Westerner—and to numerous Asians. We often fail to realize that those obscure rituals, which are so attractive to us, are equally obscure to many Asians who are only familiar with the various actions associated with them and not the specific meanings. Interpreting the meanings of ritual practices is left to specialists. The layperson is generally content simply to participate. The same is true with many of the more liturgical Western religions. This can leave the Westerner disappointed. A preconception has just been broken.

Asians have not forgotten their cultures any more than members of any other societies have. They just do not often conform to the stereo-typical images held by many Westerners.

Asians also have strong preconceptions, and their stereotypical ideas of Westerners stem from the same sources as ours. With exposure to each other's cultures, preconceptions and stereotypes slowly fade away on both sides. Until that happy day, it is best for the teacher not to expect students to come up with wise, age-old Oriental dicta in class, and to grin and bear it when students ask how you can eat cheeseburgers all day, or what makes the French so romantic.

Stereotypes can also make for interesting experiences in the classroom. During one class, for example, a Chinese student mentioned that the Cantonese "will eat anything with four legs except tables and chairs." I immediately seized the opportunity to talk about eating raw oysters—which tends to nauseate most Chinese—as a lead-in for an activity on vocabulary and tonal stress to indicate disgust in English. Another student then mentioned eating dog, in an effort to turn my stomach. I knew that, contrary to popular rumor, dog was far from a favorite dish among Chinese, with the exception of soldiers trying to be macho, and a certain class of culinary exhibitionists. I decided that it would be fun to turn this one around on them.

"I've never eaten dog. Have you?"

A few giggles and then a silence followed by a very definite "No!" from the girls—this class was made up of students in their mid-teens—and a chorus of "Not yet!" from the boys.

"Do you know a place that sells dog? I would like to try it." Dog restaurants are actually rare.

This was followed by uncomfortable whispering and then a strong chorus of "NO!" from the students who thought they were off the hook.

"I do." I said.

I even went as far as to arrange a date for what I called the "Level 5 Annual Dog Feast." My students all arrived at the appointed time and place with mixed expressions of eagerness and anxiety. We had made our way to the dog establishment before I mentioned that I thought dog was very expensive and that we might want to go for "hotpot" (also called "steamboat") instead. My students agreed, and we had a nice meal. The whole exercise did not accomplish much except to show that the students were aware of the "Chinese eat dog" rumor, and were willing to live up to it, while I could show that some Americans are also willing to eat something besides cheeseburgers if given the opportunity—an exercise in accepting and breaking stereotypes.

Some may consider that outing unprofessional in that I was willing to introduce my students to something considered disgusting. Yet, I did not take them out to eat raw oysters. That would have been considered really disgusting.

If anything was learned by our little outing, it was that we should realize that stereotypes are not always bad, and students should realize that they are not always true.

Limits

You can joke with your students and enjoy outside-of-class activities as long as you understand the limits.

In classes with Japanese students, for example, I often bring up *fugu*, which is the Japanese culinary equivalent of Russian roulette, because it is prepared from the poisonous organs of the puffer fish. But taking students out for *fugu* would be crossing the line, because there is a slight chance that eating it can be fatal, and several people a year die from it. Since Asian students respect teachers to such an extent that they may act against their better judgment to express this respect, they might even accept an invitation to such a hazard. Fun is fun, but the respect of students is not something to abuse or take lightly. Remember, an activity that seems innocuous to a Westerner may be completely unacceptable to a student or that student's family. Outside activities should be chosen with care.

Even in-class activities can backfire. One of my favorite topics in class is superstition, and one of my favorite superstitions is the Chinese "coin spirit." Chinese characters are written on a sheet of paper, and a coin is placed on the sheet. The lights are turned off, and the spirit is called. Two people place their index fingers on the coin. Questions are asked, and the coin, in answer, moves to characters on the sheet, much like to letters on a Ouija board. One must pay the spirit (there are many methods) for advice given through the coin. Failure to pay one's debts to the coin spirit is said to result in disaster.

It can also be done with a plate. But unlike the benign spirit of the coin, the spirit of the plate is considered very dangerous: too dangerous for light discussion in class, as I learned when I decided to invoke it in English. The students agreed, and we wrote words, in English, on the sheet. We called the spirit, asked questions, and got our answers. The students seemed calm and interested. It was, to all appearances, an interesting and unique class. The next day, however, I was reprimanded by the director of the school, who had received several phone calls from parents. Some of the students had liked the activity so much that they went home and told their parents, who didn't. I had crossed the line.

If you are uncertain if any activity, discussion, or class trip is suitable, ask someone who will know.

The Importance of Language
As a Key to Cultural Understanding

You can only know the limits if you understand the culture, and you can only understand the culture if you know the language.

As soon as a teacher starts teaching, that teacher should start learning. At times, aspects of Asian culture will only become clear after you have a good grasp of the language. It is a premise of TEFL theory that an EFL teacher does not need to learn a host country's language in order to teach effectively. In Asia, that is a questionable premise. Teachers who do not understand the basics of everyday life in a given country will be unable to provide concrete, first-hand examples to illustrate topics discussed in class. They are then forced to rely on second-hand information and to depend on personal observations of local life that are often so distorted as to lack credibility, or resort to limiting illustrative information to the context of their home country—or another foreign country with which they are familiar—which is also a mistake. It is a fallacy that a majority of EFL students have concrete plans to study or travel abroad. While the students do have a genuine interest in Western cultures, too many examples from that unfamiliar context are bound to cause unnecessary and unproductive confusion.

Understanding the local culture and language allows you to provide convincing, intelligent examples to enhance the class. Knowing how your students would react to a situation is the only way you can be sure that the language you teach can be comprehensive and useful to them in everyday life. Besides being impossible, attempting to teach EFL students to be photocopies of native speakers makes learning the language a chore equal to the "repeat after me and don't ask questions" methods of yesteryear. (There are some cases, however, in which the rote method is useful. These will be discussed later.)

Also, knowing the grammatical structure of your students' language can be a primary aid in understanding their problems with English. The root of most problems for EFL students is that certain grammatical aspects of English, such as tenses, do not exist in their own language, while other features of their language are not found in English.

Misunderstanding is often caused by a difference in meaning between a word used in one language and its counterpart in another. A Chinese student might say "The parts used in this product are standard," when she wants to say, "The parts used in this product are of the highest standard." The word "standard" often connotes "commonplace" or "mediocre" in English, whereas in Chinese its primary meaning is "high standard," with the other meanings being secondary.

Thais have problems with the words "convenient" and "comfortable." The explanation is easy enough. The latter means "at rest in mind or body," the former means, "easy to use." But the difference between the counterparts of these words in Thai is not so clear-cut.

Other problems are easily caught by a knowledge of Asian "yes" and "no" usage. In positive questions such as "Are you going?" The answer is the same in English and most Asian languages: "Yes, (I am)," or "No, (I am not)." But with negative questions, "Aren't you going?", we get answers like, "Yes, I am not going," or "No, I am going." These answers are intended to express agreement with what we ask. So if we were to ask a student, "You didn't come to class yesterday, did you?" She might reply, "Yes," to agree that she didn't come. It would be easy for the teacher to mistake confusion for incomprehension. The positive, "Were you absent yesterday?" is preferable. Any time negative questions come up in class, be assured that you will spend the rest of the class period trying to explain them (start by explaining that the answer is the same in both cases. This might help: Are/Aren't you going?).

We also run into a problem with some positive questions, such as:

Do you mind if I sit here?

We get answers like:

Yes you can.   No, you can't.

These seem more reasonable than:

No, I don't.   Yes, I do.

Knowledge of Asian languages can also help with understanding lower-level students who tend to rely on their own phonetic alphabets when using English—this is especially true of Japanese and Thais. The reply to "What is this?" is something like "Dizu esu a booku" in the Japanese case, or "Dis it a book" in the Thai case, and it is a big help knowing what consonantal gremlins we are dealing with if we plan to exterminate them properly. Although there is a Chinese phonetic alphabet, it is mainly used with computers and in books for small children. Chinese learn new words by being told how they sound (I know this well from my own studies). The lack of a widely used phonetic alphabet may be a plus for Chinese when studying English because they rely on the English alphabet rather than falling back on their own. Indonesian has a relatively simple grammar, and as a result, English grammar can seem incomprehensible to some Indonesian students. Knowledge of Indonesian will help the teacher understand the obstacles English can present.

New teachers are often shocked when presented with the writing of some Asian students. It may have only a slight resemblance to English, for the simple reason that it is not written in English. English vocabulary is used but the grammar is local. These teachers then try to correct the work when it would be better simply to write, "Try this again using ENGLISH grammar." After this blunt reminder, the second attempt will generally be much improved. If you do not understand the local language it is more difficult to differentiate between legitimate grammar mistakes and a complete lack of attempt to apply English grammar. Of course, some teachers can perform quite well without knowing a word of any language but their own. But for most of us, even a basic knowledge of the students' native language can provide valuable insight into learning problems mentioned above, while a reasonable degree of fluency will furnish many ideas for making classes more effective and enjoyable.

Using English or the Local Language

Knowing the language of the country is useful, but should it be spoken in class? The official party line regarding this question is "No, never." This might lead the more cynical of us to believe that the "official party" only knows English, because it is a rare teacher who speaks the students' language but never uses it with them. A more reasonable answer would be "Yes, sometimes." Feel free to use the students' language in order to save time when using a single word will explain something that would otherwise require drawings, charts and graphs, photos, and a panel of independent experts. Such words do often come up, partly because some writers of EFL/ESL textbooks seem to derive a perverse pleasure out of including vocabulary in low-level texts that could not possibly be explained through simple words or gestures.

The local language can also be used in before- or after-class discussion that is conceptually far above the current English level of the students. For instance, when I needed some background on physics theories related to interstellar space travel for a science fiction story, a physicist in one of my classes was able to provide the information, but not in English.

An experienced teacher will rarely find a need to use local languages in upper-level classes. It can be useful, however, to let students know you do understand it in order to discourage too-frequent use of their native language among themselves in class.

But Will They Use It Outside Class?

The main point of an EFL class is to provide a setting for students to use English with the teacher and with each other. Many students need the motivation supplied by a teacher in order to speak English among themselves. They generally find it embarrassing to speak English among themselves outside of class—except with foreigners. Some even suggest that others will think they are insane if they are heard speaking English in public. This is, however, subject to trends. Teenagers in most Asian countries mix English words and phrases into the local language. In the late 1980s, many Japanese pop songs contained a mix of Japanese and English. In the words of a Japanese friend, "This made Japanese pop unique in that it could be understood by nobody." Usually this localized English only serves to promote incorrect usage.

Thai/English jokes have been popular in Thailand, and some of these are clever. "What fish has two faces?" The answer is "tuna." ("Na" means "face" in Thai.)

"English only" sections in parks were popular in China during the 1980s. Groups of students would get together and speak English to one another. This phenomenon struck me as more of a harmless form of fashionable rebellion than an educational endeavor. (If, however, all the men hiding behind trees with video cameras were any indication, the central government did not take the same view of these gatherings.)

The local language should only be used to expedite the learning process. If your ability at it is limited, it is far more likely that students will understand something said in good English than in a bad version of the local language. It is also not wise to embarrass yourself by struggling to speak a simple sentence in the local language only to have it come out sounding like the incomprehensible ramblings of a deranged local infant when a single word in English would have sufficed. The EFL classroom is under no circumstances a venue for the English teacher to receive language lessons from students. Students who are subjected to this quickly begin to wonder what they are paying for.

The Students Must Come First

The students must get valid learning from the time and money they invest. If you simply ask a series of questions and expect students to supply the answer, you are teaching for yourself (kill-time-get-paid-go-home).

It is easy to use up a couple hours of class by asking students questions about their country, and they will be more than happy to supply the answers. But they will find it tedious to be required to answer seemingly pointless questions from a teacher who does not know the answers and cannot help them explain things in a reasonably eloquent way. As we all know from our own schooling, it is a rare teacher who asks a question without knowing the answer. EFL students expect the same consideration. If they are unable to supply a grammatically correct reply to a question, they expect an answer to be forthcoming from the teacher. (Remember, one goal of many EFL students is to be able to talk comprehensibly about their country to visitors.) One role of an EFL teacher is to help them accomplish that.

Unfortunately, the amount of preparation involved in teaching a class in which every base will be covered is extremely time consuming, and most language schools do not pay teachers for doing extensive preparation. Obviously, the more time a teacher spends teaching, the less time is required for preparation, and constructive classes can easily be pulled out of your "bag of tricks."

Less experienced teachers can use the technique commonly used to prepare an essay of narrowing a topic to avoid having lessons drift off on irrelevant tangents. This will help to focus the lesson and cut down on preparation time. A one-hour class about "food," or a one-page essay on "government," are useless assignments. "Ordering food" could conceivably be covered in a one-hour class, depending on the level. It might be necessary, however, to narrow the topic even more to "ordering lunch," so that the basic vocabulary and structures can be covered and reviewed during future lessons on "food-related English."

Well-focused lessons like these require minimal preparation, and they provide the students with clearly organized content that they can understand and retain. These classes work well for both the students and the teacher as they accomplish the intended purpose without being overwhelming.

The Teacher as a Game Show Host

There is considerable variety among Asian EFL students at language schools. To some, the class is only a form of constructive entertainment. The last thing they want is to walk into class and face a dull lecture. Others are far more serious. Consequently, teachers must often be able both to entertain and to educate. Games are one answer, even if they make you feel like a cross between Monty Hall and a fifth-grade math teacher. The game show host comparison is appropriate because that type of personality is very close to what Asian EFL students want in an EFL teacher.

Our problem is further complicated because many games are not as productive a means of learning as the material in the textbook or course outline. Students soon realize that they are not really accomplishing anything and feel cheated by a teacher who is only trying to please them.

There are several ways out of this quandary, and they can either be used independently or together as the situation warrants.

The first method is to try good warm-up activities at the beginning of class, game-type closing activities at the end of class, and a standard lesson in the interim, with longer games planned only occasionally.

The other method involves disguising otherwise tedious material in a game format. (These techniques are summarized in the appendix.) I have found that one of the most difficult activities to get through in a lower-level EFL class is reading passages of several paragraphs or more. Theoretically, the point of these exercises is to improve reading comprehension by having students read a text in order to distinguish the main points from peripheral details. In practice, the students want to know the meaning of every word in a passage, and they are not satisfied with being told that understanding every word is not necessary.

Conversation classes focus on speaking and listening, not reading. Long reading passages bog down the lesson, and present an obstacle.

There are several ways to deal with this:

(1) Have the students read the paragraph aloud in a sentence-by-sentence or paragraph-by-paragraph "around the room" exercise; (2) Have the students read it to each other; (3) Assign it for homework; (4) Have the students read it silently, or read it aloud yourself. None of these methods are very exciting for the students or the teacher. Such exercises can, however, become more bearable and interesting when disguised as a game.

Choose either the first or last paragraph of the text, whichever has the most relevant information. (The rest of the text can be dealt with by one of the methods above, depending on which paragraph you chose, either before or after the game.) Place the desks on opposite sides of the room and pair the students off. One student is the "reader" and the other student is the "writer." The reader must read parts of the paragraph on his or her side of the room and then go across the room to relay the information to the writer. The writer must write down the information as quickly and accurately as possible. No communication can take place without crossing a point set in the middle of the room. Naturally, the reader cannot take his or her book across the line. After the information has been exchanged, the teacher then collects the papers from the writers and distributes them randomly to the other teams for correction from the original passage. The students are usually cold-blooded with their corrections, and the results can be entertaining. This activity can be made even more difficult by using three students: a reader, a runner, and a writer.

Other "game show"–type activities can also be used in class. There is a popular game show in Thailand in which the contestants are required to guess a word by gestures and hints given by their teammates. A series of ten words appears on a screen in front of the contestant doing the describing, and points are given according to the number of words that are guessed correctly per minute. The "describer" has the option of "passing" a word that proves too difficult to elucidate. This is especially useful in classes of mixed ability. Another game that follows the same format requires participants to "draw" a word on a whiteboard.

Activities like these are excellent for EFL students. Valuable practice with the language takes place within a familiar format that everyone enjoys. The students usually already know the rules, so little time is wasted in explaining the game. Teachers in other countries should make it a point to watch popular game shows and adapt them for use in the classroom.

Student Expectations

In addition to entertaining students, teachers in Asia will encounter other expectations that go a bit beyond what they can reasonably fulfill.

These are generally voiced as "requests for a little help" by students who need assistance in some work- or school-related project. Of course, there is no harm in taking a quick look at some homework or helping with the translation of a short letter. Beware: a "little help" can often be much more than that.

A teacher in Taiwan was asked by his boss to do a favor for a friend who wanted help with correcting "a few" mistakes in his masters thesis. The teacher agreed, assuming that anyone capable of finishing a paper on that academic level could write fairly well, and that any corrections would only take a couple of hours.

The teacher soon realized his mistake. The thesis was about 30 pages long, and absolutely incomprehensible. After an attempt at reading it, my friend decided that it couldn't be a thesis—he couldn't even figure out the topic—but a thesis proposal of some kind. He declared the paper unsalvageable, and returned it to his boss.

When asked what the paper was, my friend's boss replied that it was indeed a thesis, and that it had been written by his nephew. He said that if my friend could just correct some mistakes it would be sufficient.

Not wanting to get on the bad side of his boss, he spent several evenings completely rewriting the paper—no easy task as it was not in any language that he had previously encountered and its actual topic remained in doubt.

The teacher handed over the newly written essay only to have the nephew return it because it was not on the topic about which he thought he had written. The boss asked him for one more try but he refused, stating that other commitments would require most of his time for the next several weeks.

Nothing more was said about the paper until the boss mentioned that his nephew had received his degree. He had decided to change his topic and submit the paper that my friend had "helped correct."

Not only was a significant amount of time spent on a project for which there was no compensation, but the "favor" ended up being unethical. It would have been better to have written, "Try this again using ENGLISH grammar" on the thing, and given it back.

These "little favors" asked by students—and colleagues—can add up. It is best to relegate questions and assistance not directly related to class work to a few minutes after the end of each class period.

The Teacher as a Person

Keeping professional and private life separate is essential for teachers in Asia. The amount of attention you receive in public life makes you cherish your private time. Limits should be set in the beginning to ensure that you will retain your original enthusiasm for teaching and enjoy your off hours to the utmost.

Those who teach private classes in their homes can find themselves getting late-night phone calls, unscheduled visits, and the like from students, usually business people, with an "emergency question" that often proves very time-consuming to answer. In order to set limits and provide structure, it is a good idea to hold an "open house" night a few times a month to offer personal assistance. This can prove popular with students, while allowing some control over your time, and it can also lead to more paid private tutorials.

Sometimes teachers are offered free room and board from a family or individual in exchange for "occasional" English lessons. This is economical, but it may leave you with minimal privacy. A teacher may also be regarded by his or her host family as a "walking dictionary." Remember, the word "alone" connotes "lonely" in many Asian languages, and the Asian home is considered a place for a kind of continual interaction that the Westerner may not be accustomed to and may find confining. Homestay arrangements are more practical for the short-term visitor to Asia who is looking for maximum intercultural contact in a short period of time. Those who plan to teach in Asia long-term will appreciate the freedom that private accommodation, and a private life, offers.

Talking About Money

Unfortunately, one of the aspects of teaching English in Asia is a necessity to discuss, and negotiate, payment for your services as a teacher. In universities and language centers, this is not often a problem as the institution will generally state a wage that the teacher is free to accept or reject—along with the job. The wages offered by universities are often set by the government or a board of directors, and they are often standardized. Language centers often offer a starting salary that is determined by the director's feeling about the teacher's experience and other relevant factors. Raises are often based on seniority rather than merit. Nevertheless, those who are popular with students will often find that they are given more classes at better times.

Most teachers accept private students to supplement their income. Teaching privately requires negotiation of wages as well as other aspects of the arrangement. You will need to set rules regarding class postponements and cancellations, consultations outside of class, transportation allowances, and payment for textbooks and other materials. Students often begin private classes with the best of intentions, only to lose interest as other commitments or activities arise. This can leave you with a big hole in your schedule and no compensation. As problems with private arrangements tend to affect the teacher more than the student, it is wise to decide on a set policy regarding private work and stick to it without exception.

You should charge a higher rate than the hourly wage offered by language centers and you should require a predetermined number of hours to be paid for in advance, with the stipulation that if a student cancels a class without notice (generally 24 hours) full payment for that class will be due anyway. This rule is essential because many private students do tend to cancel at the drop of a hat. Make clear that any textbooks you introduce are not included in the hourly rate and must be paid for separately (I charge for my copy and theirs), as must any outside activities such as meals or excursions.

Once a relationship develops between a teacher and a student, the student will often forget that the teacher is trying to make a living and will expect "special consideration" regarding fees or other aspects of the agreement. You can state that, although you agree that the student is "special" and does deserve special consideration, you must work during work hours and that your free time is limited and often consumed by other commitments. This tends to put things in their proper perspective and saves you from having inconvenient, and expensive, holes punched in your schedule.

In some parts of Asia, particularly Southeast Asia, English is still undervalued and the teacher will be forced to bargain for a reasonable salary. This will require you to use related experience, travel time, and inconvenient schedules to your advantage while the student will use lack of time and money to his or hers. This type of bargaining is understandably unattractive to many teachers, as it seems unethical to haggle over the price of education. Nevertheless, this ritual is important in many Asian societies (except Japan, generally). It is essential to go about it amiably but firmly, always keeping in mind that you are a better judge of the value of your time than are any potential students.

The role of negotiator is just one of the many functions associated with teaching EFL in Asia. Expertise in this area comes with practice, and you may even eventually begin to enjoy it.

So How Do I Know If I'm Doing the Right Thing?

You can judge your value as a teacher by the attitudes of those with whom you interact: students, colleagues, and administrators. As a means of self-evaluation, you could ask:

Are my students happy to see me each day? Do I truly enjoy what I am doing? Am I working as many hours as my seniority warrants? Am I being paid enough to live the way I like? Are my students making progress? Am I making progress? Am I accepted by the people I work with? Do I feel comfortable in class? Am I making an attempt to understand my students, their culture, and their language? Am I open-minded? Am I patient? Am I presenting a quality product?

If the answer to all the questions above is "yes," then you are surely doing the right thing. The following section, "The Student," is a personal look at average East Asian students of English: their goals, motivations, and fears about learning English from a native speaker. It will provide cultural insights and offer further useful suggestions for the classroom as well as for everyday life.

THREE

The Student

Student/Teacher Relationships

The previous section outlined what is expected of the EFL teacher in East Asia. Here we will have a look at what teachers can expect from their students. In general, teachers enjoy a high status in Asian society, and as noted earlier, they are often treated with much respect by the majority of their students. The Westerner, however, is not really considered to be a full-fledged member of society and is often expected to be ignorant of local customs. One's knowledge is considered important, but the simple fact that one is a foreigner will cause surprising reactions among students.

Most Asian students have not had much direct contact with Westerners other than tourists. When interacting with Western teachers they are often torn between behaving as they have been taught throughout their lives and acting in a manner that they think the teacher will consider appropriate. What a student believes to be an appropriate interaction with a Westerner could range from absolutely correct to completely wrong, depending on that student's level of sophistication and the amount of experience he or she has had with Westerners. When students choose to act as they have been taught, the tables turn, and the Westerner is left with the problem of working out what is proper in that culture under those particular circumstances. Results vary depending on how observant that Westerner happens to be.

The Western teacher will find that correctly responding to and using the social mannerisms that are so common in Asia can be complicated. Always leave it to the students' better judgment about how and when these gestures should be used. If given the choice, opt to use Western social mannerisms with which you are comfortable, and make a point of explaining how these gestures are used in various social settings. Many Asians find the handshake just as perplexing as the Thai *wai* is to any non-Thai. Instruction regarding its uses is relevant even in EFL classes since many students will meet Westerners in social and business settings in their own country.

In many East Asian countries, students stand and bow when a teacher enters the classroom. This is common, and it is done without a second thought. You might notice, however, when entering the classroom, an uncomfortable pause that usually ends with about two-thirds of the class standing and bowing and the other third looking around and giggling. An action that had always been automatic has just turned into a minor fiasco because a third of the class is not sure what to do when a Westerner is the teacher. Anyone would agree, however, that giggling and looking around is inappropriate even in a Western classroom setting. You are now forced either to ignore the whole situation or try to rectify it. If you choose to ignore it, you will have to cope with the same behavior during every class until the students finally come to an agreement on what is proper. You may choose to tell the students that, in the West, adult students don't do anything special when a teacher walks into the room. Since this is an English class, they should behave as Western students would.

That remedy is fine—if it works. It sometimes doesn't. If it does, the more conservative students will lose a certain amount of respect for you. You have just asked them to dispense with a deeply ingrained ritual of showing deference.

Another solution is to tell the students to go ahead and act as they would with a local teacher. Although many Westerners have an aversion to being bowed to—and I am one of them—by allowing the students to continue a ritual that makes them feel comfortable, you will have made the first step in being accepted on—almost—the same level as a local teacher. In similar situations, I have long followed the advice of a progressive Chinese teacher who also felt uncomfortable with bowing, and have told my students that they are bowing to the school and to education—not to me.

Those who are familiar with Thailand are also familiar with the *wai,* a prayer-like gesture used by Thais when greeting each other and in many other day-to-day social interactions. When and where and who to *wai* to can be very confusing for those who have not been brought up doing it. Thai students *wai* teachers when they are handed a paper, when they meet in the hall, when they enter class, when they leave class, and in many other social interactions.

Like most non-Thais, I was confused at first about when to return the *wai* (at least I knew that students *wai* first). I felt very uncomfortable with such an unaccustomed gesture. I made it a point to observe student/teacher interactions between Thais and to make note of what the Thai teacher did. I found the student/teacher *wai* ratio to be about 20 to one. To my relief, I discovered that I could pretty much limit my *wais* to social interactions and simply smile in response to the *wais* of students before and after class. I noticed that one Western teacher who had not done such careful research looked like a parody walking around "*waiing*" everything that moved.

Those who teach at language centers may not encounter any of these situations because many of their students will be veterans of similar courses who are comfortable in the "Western" setting that some centers can provide through an English-only focus and frequent class meetings. New students mimic the actions of the "old hands," and our problem is solved. At other venues, you will have to adapt your methods to your students. The much touted theory that EFL classes should be simulations of a Western environment is unrealistic in universities and other settings where classes meet only a few hours a week. Rituals are an important facet of all societies. The teacher who attempts to do away with rituals in the classroom should carefully consider the long- and short-term effects (no matter how minor) and weigh them against the debatable value of a pseudo-Western classroom environment.

Most problems of the type discussed above are the result of a cultural gap between teachers and students, easily worked out when they have a little more contact with one another.

Occasionally, you will encounter real discipline problems in class. A student may think that having a Western teacher is the funniest thing that has ever happened to him or her. Such behavior is more common in high-school or university classes where courses taught by Westerners are sometimes mandatory for all students—even those not majoring in

English. Here the majority of the students have low/medium–level English abilities and a corresponding amount of interest and motivation. This majority is subject to peer pressure from the side of the better students and that of the troublemakers. If you want to succeed in motivating these mediocre students to actually improve their English—and not just marginally pass the exam—something must be done about the discipline problems. This is an area in which we must tread carefully to avoid overstepping some often-invisible cultural boundaries.

In a freshman class at a university in Thailand, a teacher handed a homework assignment to a student who then responded with a polite *wai*. The student next to her found this quite funny and burst into laughter. Because the young woman to whom the teacher had handed the paper was an excellent student and the comedian was a bit of a troublemaker, he decided to confront the troublemaker rather than let the good student feel that she had done something wrong.

"Stand up Somchai."

The student found this to be funny too, but he did manage to get to his feet.

"Somchai thinks that being polite is funny. He is now going to tell us why."

Since the student was far below the basic level of the class, this had to be translated for him. His attitude quickly changed because he realized he was unable to manage a simple sentence in English, much less explain his actions.

The teacher then added in Thai (cueing the student that his response could also be in Thai), "If he is unable to tell us in English, he will then apologize to us for wasting our time."

The resulting apology was sincere. His attitude improved markedly, and he was able to pass the class. I hear that, although he is still a below-average student, he is now polite to his teachers.

Discipline problems can take many forms, and a less successful example of "nipping it in the bud" was related to me by a colleague teaching at an up-market private high school in Bangkok who had a problem with male students wearing cosmetics in class. While this sometimes occurs in Thai schools, many Westerners find it disconcerting. On a particularly bad day, my colleague found one of his students hiding behind his book.

"What are you doing?" He asked as he approached the student.

"Nothing."

The teacher removed the book.

"What is that!?"

"Lip gloss." was the reply.

"Isn't there something in the dress code about not wearing cosmetics?"

"That's for girls."

"I don't wear cosmetics, and when you are in this room, you won't either! Go downstairs and wash that stuff off your face!"

This little scene resulted in several complaints from parents, and a lecture on Thailand from the other teachers. The boy didn't stop wearing cosmetics, and the teacher only managed to make trouble for himself.

He had confronted the student in class—in front of other students, exactly as in the first example. Both teachers had good reasons to discipline their students, right? Not so, apparently. After mulling it over, the two teachers decided that, in the second incident, the teacher had confronted the student about something that is generally ignored by *Thai* teachers (and society) while rudeness/disrespect—the first teacher's problem—is not. He had crossed that invisible cultural line. The first teacher, by sheer luck, had done what any Thai teacher would do in order to maintain control of a class. The second had not.

In any Asian society, teachers should avoid confronting students in front of others unless it is necessary. Most minor problems can be worked out by a private discussion with the student. With experience, or by careful observation, you will see how good local teachers can maintain control without losing the harmony that is essential in maintaining a productive classroom environment.

It may take some time to get accustomed to the role of the teacher in Asia, and your students' expectations are likely to be high. In the West, teachers encourage students to point out their mistakes if the students' criticism is productive for the class as a whole. This strategy is rare in Asia. One would think that this reluctance by the students to point out mistakes would allow instructors to get away with academic murder. Nevertheless, just because teacher errors are not mentioned does not mean that they are not noticed. You may teach an activity incorrectly, ask if there are any questions, and receive none, only to find that as soon as class is dismissed half the students will approach with questions.

The students did not want to challenge you in front of the class. On the negative side, if they do not feel comfortable with you, they may bring their questions to another teacher. Too much of that can lead to obvious problems.

In countries with a strong work ethic (Japan, Taiwan) teachers are often expected to live and breathe their profession. Students (and employers) will be surprised that you are not inclined to teach an 8 a.m. class on Sunday morning or to spend your off-hours helping them with their classwork. To avoid being overburdened, and burning out, you must draw the line. Local teachers are often very good at this. In many cases, their low pay (often less than foreign teachers) makes their material status inconsistent with the high social status accorded to teachers. They must seek outside income, which limits their time to such an extent that they must organize it carefully. Many of these teachers offer paid tutorials at home for students who want them and schedule set times for essential meetings with students at school. (Some, however, do go a bit overboard with their outside activities, like the teacher in Taiwan who would bring a portable TV to class so he could keep up with the stock market.)

On the Spot:
The Last Place a Student Wants to Be

Except for the occasional discipline problem, confrontations with students should be avoided, and students should not be put in situations in which they will feel uncomfortable. The worst possible feeling for an Asian student is to stand in front of classmates and be unable to answer a question shot out with no warning by the teacher. The student will feel obligated to answer, and may be extremely embarrassed if unable to form a response.

No response is the typical response in a lower-level English class in Asia. Teachers not accustomed to it will find it infuriating. You bring up what you think is a hot topic, and ask a few questions to the class in general. No reply. You then ask individual students what they think. No reply. You write the questions on the board, and ask again. Silence. You drop the topic and sigh in frustration.

I recently walked into class and asked, "So, what do you think of the definition of 'Bangkok' in the *Longman Dictionary of Contemporary English*?" All my students knew what I was talking about because this dictionary recommended for the course was being heavily criticized in the Thai media for its definition of Bangkok as a city with more than its fair share of prostitutes. A very hot topic, to say the least.

"So what do you think?"

Silence.

I then asked one of the better students. No reply. "Talk about it with a partner and then we will discuss it as a class." BOOM! Every student in the room was talking loudly, in Thai. I waited a few minutes and then said, "Try to talk about it in English, okay?" They all laughed. After they had had time to prepare their answers, I went around the room asking individual students. "It is not fair." "It is incorrect." "It is discrim . . . uh . . . discrimin . . ." "Discriminatory?" "Yes." "It is impolite." "It is wrong." "It is true." The last brought laughter, and I did not offer my opinion. I generally don't when the topic involves something negative about the country. "What do you think?" they asked me in unison. "The same as you," I said simply. Even though the lesson plan required reading some text about the potential anti-cancer properties of kelp and how to find sentence subjects, verbs, and objects in that enlightening document, I went with the flow and continued the lesson with a discussion of ways to reply to ridicule and criticism.

Students need time to prepare answers. Otherwise, they will feel put on the spot, and respond poorly, if at all. The more important the question, the more time will be needed to prepare an answer, which creates long, ineffective pauses in class. A useful teaching technique is to slowly decrease the amount of time students are given to prepare answers, so that they will eventually be able to answer questions spontaneously. This can be accomplished by leaving as big a time gap as needed between asking a question and calling a student's name at the beginning of the term, and slowly closing that gap during the term until (hopefully) students can quickly answer questions. If you are lucky, another teacher will have already done this job. You can test the extent of your students' abilities by seeing how they respond to statements:

"I had a great day yesterday."

Silence.

If the students respond with, "Oh really? What happened?"—this is highly unlikely—rest assured that you have a class that can respond well to any conversational gambit and work from there.

A very effective questioning technique is called "Ask-Pause-Call"

(APC). The teacher asks a question, pauses, and then calls a student's name. The attention of all the students is focused, and they all have time to work out the answer. If you call the student's name first, most of the others will "switch off" and not pay attention because they know they won't be called on. This technique takes several class periods to perfect, but it is an excellent way to avoid putting students on the spot.

Shyness and Peer Pressure

Students' reluctance to speak is one of the main gripes of teachers in East Asia. New teachers are often surprised at how quiet a class—especially the first one—can be. I have seen new teachers confidently walk into a new class only to walk out again shaking their heads. Once, it was only a half hour and the teacher was crying.

"That's not quite what I expected," is the typical first statement a teacher makes after facing a mute class. The statements that follow are more specific in addition to being unprintable. Usually the teacher will have prepared a nice introduction, leaving plenty of room for an expected bombardment of questions from the students. Unfortunately, the bombardment turned out to be a single shot, probably from the most outgoing student, along the lines of, "Do you like Japanese food?" The stress starts while you are trying to figure out what to do with the next 47 minutes, and it increases with every second thereafter.

Students in a new class are just as uncomfortable with each other as they are with the teacher. Ice needs to be broken all around, and a long introduction from a teacher with unfamiliar speech patterns and pronunciation tends to be more confusing than productive. Speakers of tonal languages also have a "tonal ear," and variations in accent can throw even higher-level students off until they have had a chance to let it sink in. Teacher-talk should be kept to an absolute minimum during new classes. Student-centered activities should be used heavily in order to let the students get to know each other and become accustomed to the teacher. Obviously, it is necessary to give your name and a few words of introduction, but other personal information is best presented gradually as part of an activity.

One sure-fire first activity is an around-the-room (see note on seating in the "The Class") exercise in which the teacher says his or her name; then the student to the right of the teacher repeats the teacher's name and his or her own name; the next student says the teacher's name, and that of the preceding student, and then his or her name, and so on. Continue around the room until the last student has to recite everybody's name. Then, reverse the direction to surprise those students on the right side who thought that they had gotten off easily. This will finally leave the teacher to recite the names of all the students in the class. Chinese students (in Taiwan and, to a lesser extent, in the PRC) tend to take English nicknames for use in class, which makes this an easy task for the teacher and a more difficult one for the students. In other parts of Asia, there will usually be a list of 20 names or nicknames in a foreign language, the reciting of which is sure to be embarrassing enough to have the students falling out of their chairs laughing. Besides breaking the ice, this activity allows you to hear each name twice—unless the students catch on—giving you the chance to associate a name with a face and double-check it. Remembering students' names is essential for the usual reasons (checking roll and grading). Hearing the teacher use their name in class makes students feel just a little bit "special." It confirms to them that the teacher is concerned with their individual progress. I have gotten many notes from students "thanking" me for remembering their names.

One good follow-up to the "name game" is a variation of the "stand up and introduce yourself" activity used in the past. Many teachers find that asking a student to stand up in front of a class full of strangers and make a self-introduction is of limited value. It only gets formalities out of the way while putting students on the spot. Although introducing oneself is an important facet of daily life, very few like to do it in front of a group. In the following more realistic activity, students can meet one another, and then introduce their partners to the group.

Put the students in pairs. (Sod's law says every class will have an uneven number of students. In that case, the extra student should be put with one of the pairs—leaving the teacher free to circulate.) Tell them to find out various things about their partner. Lower-level classes will need to be helped along, so the questions should be written on the board. In higher levels a list of topics (family, hobbies, sports, likes/dislikes) is sufficient. Warn students that they will be expected to introduce their partners at the end of class. This activity gives the students a chance to prepare what they will say, get to know each other, and talk about someone besides themselves.

An alternative to "partners introduction" is to try an old favorite:

"Find someone who . . ."

Prepare a handout that looks like this:

FIND SOMEONE WHO   NAME OF PERSON:

    plays tennis

    has never eaten pizza

    has their own bedroom

    has been abroad

    has been bitten by a dog

    is not from _____

    was born in June

    hates to do housework

    has an interesting pet

Tell the students to stand up and circulate until they have found someone who fits each description. Use your own questions for the handout and make them general enough that the students will not have too much trouble finding names. One question that obviously only applies to you can be included to encourage students to approach you.

These activities are excellent ice-breakers. They give students a chance to get to know each other. They also promote an informal atmosphere by getting the students out of their seats and moving around. Once the students have become acquainted, you may find that they are far more outgoing than they first appeared.

Once in a while, you will come across a class that is extremely reluctant to speak. In these cases, always present the exercise/topic/activity without pushing too hard for a response. Put the students in pairs to work it out, and then elicit answers from the class and from individual students. Error correction should be done tactfully by getting a consensus and then correcting the group as a whole instead of individually.

Drills and rote recitation also work well in these classes, as the students are familiar with these methods and are not resistant to them as are Western students. Use any method at your disposal to get students to speak as a group, and wait until after this procedure before expecting responses from individuals. Once you can get the class to speak together, the more outgoing students will begin to stand out. Direct individual questions at them. Their answers will set an example for the rest of the class.

There is a larger percentage of chronically shy students in Asia than in Western countries. These students can usually function adequately in daily life because the condition is common enough that it is accepted by society at large. These individuals have a very difficult time in English conversation classes and will usually drop out. Giving them the individual attention they need is not often possible, and it is generally better for the majority if they do drop. Shy students don't cope well with the pressure of being continually required to speak out, and they slow the pace of the class. After all, not everyone is cut out to learn a foreign language.

Conversely, shy students can be surprising in that they can also be very good learners. They are just very low-key about it. These students may not want to speak out. If that is the case—so be it. Let them learn in the way that they feel most comfortable. A teacher can tell if such a student is learning by listening to his or her pair-work activities (pair-work is explained in "The Class"). They can usually do these and other "low-pressure" activities well.

Crossing the Bridge Between Guest and Teacher

Long-term teachers in East Asia may eventually find themselves feeling as if they are being perpetually treated as a guest in the home of an intimate friend.

Most Asian societies pride themselves on being excellent hosts. The hospitality that Asians are renowned for often produces glowing reports from those who have taught there short-term. Those who have lived there for longer periods of time will have varying opinions—depending on how well they have been able to actively adapt—ranging from critical to enthusiastic.

Given the Asian predilection to present a good host image, and the desire of Westerners to accept the good guest role, we arrive at a sort of harmony. But for how long? Doesn't a guest wear out his or her welcome after a certain amount of time? Don't the formalities involved in being a guest eventually become tedious? Do you realistically see yourself as able to be a guest—even in your classroom—for the next ten years—or for the rest of your life? How intimately must you know East Asia to be accepted on equal terms?

Active adaptation involves following the steps outlined in the previous section, along with realizing that you will always be thought of as a guest by society in general. Yet, in the classroom, and among those with whom you interact on a daily basis, you can at least work toward the goal of being accepted as what you are: teacher first, and foreigner second. When students realize that you are not culturally ignorant, they will make it evident by dropping the "host façade" to the point that classroom discussions will not always dwell on the pros of their society, but also the cons. Students will seek advice on problems that are not limited to English, but also on matters of a local nature about which you are known to be well informed.

If you do your homework, you may find that certain individuals will accept you as an "honorary" member of society by treating you as if you were just a regular person. This acceptance, however, will be the result of much linguistic, sociological, cultural, historical, and psychological research. There are no shortcuts, and you will still have to prove yourself—indirectly, of course—to new people with whom you interact every day. "I am not a tourist," is declared by thousands of tourists in thousands of places in Asia every day. The standard, non-stated, reply to that declaration is, "Why not?"

The long-term and complex process of adaption is illustrated by an old story about an elephant that walked up to a man and said, "I am not an elephant."

"Why not?" the man asked.

"Because I can ride a bicycle," the elephant said. The elephant then hopped on a bicycle and rode away.

"That elephant can ride a bicycle," the man said to his friend who was nearby.

A few weeks later, the elephant cycled up to the man again and said, "I am not an elephant."

"Why not?" the man asked again.

"Because I can read a newspaper."

"Smart elephant," the man thought as the elephant began to read out loud.

The elephant then went deep into the city to intensely study the ways of humans. After years of studying the habits of the human race, he eventually became so comfortable with people that he felt he no longer needed to prove himself. He still looked like an elephant—there was no way he could change that—but he had adapted to the human race so well that his lifestyle was now identical.

One day, on the way to the tailor, the elephant rode past the man with whom he had spoken so many years before. The man looked up from the card game he was playing and commented to his friend, "that man rides a bicycle just like an elephant."

An Illogical Look at Logic

A frequent topic of discussions among teachers in Asia is the seeming lack of logic among students, and in the society as a whole. Many actions of students are seen to have no logical basis, appearing unreasonable to their Western teachers.

While working at a language center in Taiwan that was located on the tenth floor of an office building, I was often so perplexed by the way the Chinese used elevators that I would bring it up in class.

The building housed a department store on the first three floors, and several language centers on the upper floors. Before classes, the elevators would always be very busy with people getting on at both the first floor and basement levels. My tight schedule allowed only a few minutes to get from a class in a nearby building to a class on the tenth floor of that building.

I would wait for the elevator on the first floor, and, without fail, if the elevator was on an upper floor, someone would push the "DOWN" button. This often caused minor delays, but I was more interested in finding out why someone would push a button to go down when he or she was invariably going up.

According to my students, some people feel that it is logical to push the down button in order to make the elevator come DOWN to them.

"That seems irregular, " I said.

"Why?" they asked.

"Well . . . uh . . . hmmmm . . If a button is pushed on the first floor, it only follows that the person pushing that button is there too, right?"

What this and other related notions imply is that what is considered to be logic can depend entirely on one's perspective, and the structure of one's culture in general.

Members of societies in which individualism is the norm tend to think in terms of "democratic equalitarian logic," which is individualistic in nature but places strict limits on the right to infringe on another person. It is, therefore, somewhat objective in that it accepts that what may be good for society as a whole may not be good for the individual. In order to meet the needs of the individual it must consider the demands of society as a whole—along with all related facts—without regard to social status. This type of logic generally follows the tenets of "scientific logic" in that it emphasizes weighing of evidence and it seems sensible to those who adhere to it.

Those in more homogeneous cultures (most Asian societies) tend to think in terms of a more autocratic logic that is hierarchical in nature and tends to forego the rights of the individual in favor of those of the group. While trying to satisfy the needs of dissimilar groups within the society, the direction of society as a whole is lost. It does not follow the rules of "scientific logic" in that the correctness of one's opinion is based solely on one's position in the hierarchy, and contrary evidence is considered to be bothersome and is not taken into consideration. Again, to those who adhere to it, it seems reasonable.

The discussion above is my interpretation of a theory presented in Richard W. Hartzell's *Harmony in Conflict* (Taipei: Caves Books, 1988). Hartzel's idea of "arbitrary logic" is an excellent first step in understanding why many things are done the way they are in Asia. This type of "non-Euclidian" logic is worth considering for anyone who has ever asked, "Why do they do that?"

An interest in arbitrary logic has often led me to present exercises in logic to my classes, as I find it fascinating that students who excel in mathematical logic have such a difficult time with logical problems when they are placed in a linguistic format. Consider the following problem presented to an intermediate-level English conversation class to solve:

Three women, Anne, Betty, and Cindy often have lunch together.

1. Each orders coffee or tea after lunch.

2. If Anne orders coffee, then Betty orders the drink that Cindy orders.

3. If Betty orders coffee, then Anne orders the drink that Cindy does not order.

4. If Cindy orders tea, then Anne orders the drink that Betty orders.

Who always orders the same drink after lunch? What is the drink? How do you know?

(These exercises were based on an activity in *Speaking* by Roger Gower, Oxford University Press: 1987.)

I often present this exercise as a special activity and the students usually have a lot of trouble with it until I tell them to work it out mathematically as A, B, and C. When approached in mathematical terms, it is solved quickly—often with the students correcting my explanation.

Before the exercise I usually write the word "logical" on the board, explain its meaning and then ask the students if it applies to them. After they solve the problem, I say, "Yes, you are logical," explain the problem to those who didn't get it, and move on.

Most of the students in this particular class were enrolled in private high schools where they excelled. They were extremely clever, and they even managed to get me turned around during my explanation. One student in particular really confused me, and then politely led me out of it when he realized that I was lost—at times I think I could be outdone in math by any reasonably intelligent elementary-school student. I then congratulated the student on being more logical than his teacher, and quickly moved on to a comforting grammar exercise.

Just as I thought I had moved safely away from the formulas that were covering the board—English words were left behind as soon as I had told the students to think mathematically—a student raised his hand. (Students raising hands is becoming more common in Asia. In the past, students either spoke as a group or waited to be called on by the teacher.)

"Why is that logical? I think Cindy is logical because she does what she wants to."

"The answer is logical because it is the only possible answer to this problem," I said.

"Never mind," he said.

The next day, I received two unsolicited essays. One was from the only older woman in the class, of mainly high school students. Her letter presented a theory—with no basis—on why it was possible that one of the women always ordered two drinks. She said that Betty always ordered two drinks because Cindy was her friend and Anne was her boss. Betty couldn't order coffee without upsetting Cindy, and she couldn't order tea without upsetting Anne. Her solution was to order both coffee and tea. She could thereby avoid offending both her friend and her boss. Her report showed total incomprehension of the question. It was, however, a fine example of how arbitrary logic looks when it is used in a situation in which scientific logic is the only possible means of finding a reasonable answer. I simply corrected the grammatical mistakes on the paper and returned it to her.

The second essay came from the student who had asked the question at the end of the activity. I present his essay here exactly as I received it from him—with no grammatical corrections.

Who Is Logical?

Before this question, "Anne, Betty, and Cindy often eat lunch together," you said that the person who could answer or find the answer was logical. Me, I want to know too if I'm logical but after you told the man who answered correctly (following the quiz book) was logical, that's not clear so I would like to tell you my reason. I don't want to change your mind or make you believe me and tell me "Oh! You're logical!" This paper is just for to show you my reason and idea.

I found the same answer (but different type to find it) that Cindy always orders the same drink after lunch that is "tea." *(Anne is actually the answer to the exercise).* From the story, Cindy doesn't interest or follow the other's order, she has her own taste (idea) so she drinks or does the way she likes. This reason why I choose her. If I have some problems, I need someone reasonable and confident whom I can consult with or who can point me the way out but not someone who hasn't his own idea (like Anne or Betty).

Your question came from the book, the answer too so we should follow it but not me. I found that everyone (in the class) might have the same type to find an answer like you, they probably learned from school or someone taught them. Me too, I have remembered this type from school but it was non sense for me. Your book isn't my mother. I came from my mother but it doesn't mean that I have to agree with her. When you were born, who was teaching you speak, sing, walk, run and who fed you but when you're growing up and become mature, I think you have your own world.

I wonder if your parents, your teachers or your textbooks are more important than your experiences. For me, they're something valuable in my life but they aren't my everything so I always have my own decision except sometimes because I'm not Superman.

After your question, everyone wants to be logical man so they're serious. To tell you the truth, at first I would like to tell you "It's not my business to find who orders the same drink after lunch." But when I started really working and listened carefully an answer at the end, I found that "Who is logical" didn't work anything!

That essay was more than a once-in-a-career gem. It was proof that I had been able to—albeit unintentionally—generate enough emotion in a student to get a passionate reaction—in English! I infer from his essay that this student was rebelling against the group—of which he considered my book and me to be the leader. So here is an individual refusing to accept elements of both perspectives of logic outlined above. Others will have different interpretations of this episode, but I think all will agree that, since the two people who did not fit into the group were the only individuals who refused to accept the answer, there is a struggle going on as to what "kind" of logic is most practical in Asian society.

My reply to his essay was, "Scientific logic (what I was talking about) and 'individualism' (what you were talking about) are both personality traits that have as little in common as 'punctuality' and 'heroism.' Grammatically, your essay was one of the best I have ever received from a student at your level of English ability, and I appreciate your taking the time to express your feelings. I suggest that you take a look at the two words in a good dictionary and perhaps their meanings—and the purpose of my activity—will become clearer." A bit harsh, but he had been in my classes on and off for months; I knew he would understand.

One well-known logic activity (a riddle, actually) requires a very good grasp of the English language. None of my students have ever been able to work out the answer to the following riddle. Maybe one of yours can:

> A man walking to the city comes to a fork in the road. He doesn't know which of the two roads leads to the city so he must ask one of two boys who are sitting there. One boy always lies, and the other boy always tells the truth. The man can only ask one question. What question should he ask?

That riddle will require some drawing on the board to make the situation clear. The answer, "What would your friend say if I asked him which road goes to the city?" (and do the opposite of what he says), will also need some explaining.

> A final riddle that some students do solve is a variation of an old one about two planes. One is flying from Tokyo to Singapore at a speed of 537 miles an hour, and the other is flying from Singapore to Tokyo at 483 miles per hour, because it is facing a headwind. Which plane will be closer to Singapore when they meet? (If your students can figure it out, so can you.)

Logic activities in class can be enjoyable for the teacher and the class. The answers, and the methods the students use to find them, can provide the teacher with insight into the ways that members of a culture go about problem solving and analysis. Students consider these activities to be an enjoyable way to check their comprehension of a text (the problem) and a challenging test of their communication skills (explaining the answer). It is possible, however, that the unexpected will happen (as with my student's viewpoint and related essay) or that at the end of class you will find yourself rubbing your temples and mumbling, "Why do they do that?"

Face: Not So Hard to Understand

Another reason that we may ask, "Why do they . . .?" is not related to perceptions of logic but to a concept that is far more abstract: face. Visitors to Asia are often perplexed by this concept, and many tend to disregard it as another factor involved in the so-called "Eastern Enigma." In fact, Westerners are familiar with face and lose it, give it, and receive it every day.

Most of us have some embarrassing memory, like the time that we jumped into the swimming pool only to find our swimsuit had fallen down around our ankles, or when we spilled a drink in our lap, or how the teacher called us a nitwit in trig class. We lost face.

And we have positive ones too: we arrived at a party wearing exactly the right thing, or when we drove an uncle's Porshe to school, or when we won the science contest with our cow-dung-powered washing machine. We gained face.

"What a pretty dress!" is face for the wearer as well as the one who gave the compliment—it shows mutual good taste. Although public comments about dress tend to embarrass Asians (especially Japanese), these compliments are an integral aspect of Western face-giving.

As in Western societies, face is gained by anything that shows an individual in a good light in front of anybody. But in Asia, that can encompass a much wider sphere.

In Asia, the actions of others can be just as important as one's own. It is a rare Westerner who would feel a loss of face in being seen in public with an inappropriately dressed acquaintance. In Asia, however, it would be. Dress, manner, and actions all reflect on the individual and are expected to be in keeping with his or her place in society. In a student/teacher relationship, face is gained or lost by how you present yourself.

A teacher in Japan had agreed to instruct privately a student employed at a large office. It was decided that the office's conference room could be used as a classroom for the tutorials. Since the class was scheduled on a day that the teacher was otherwise free, he did not pay much attention to the clothes he wore to the session, and he often arrived in blue jeans and a T-shirt. After a few classes, the student abruptly changed the venue to a nearby restaurant. The teacher was not happy with this crowded venue, where he found it very difficult to work. He asked the student why she had changed the meeting place, and she gave no reply, but her discomfort was obvious.

After a couple more lessons, the teacher again asked about the location, and he received a reply that was atypical in its directness.

"I changed to the restaurant because of your clothes. My coworkers asked me why I had a Western bum coming to visit me. I was ashamed to tell them that you were my teacher, so I said that I was teaching you Japanese. They thought it would be better if I did that on my own time, so I take my lunch now."

The teacher was offended and the student was equally embarrassed. They did not continue with the English lessons.

When the teacher related that story to me, he said that he could understand about the clothes, but he was amazed at the student's directness.

"A typical student would have just canceled the class . . . said she was busy or something," I agreed.

"Maybe she liked the way I teach."

"I think she wanted to confront you with the problem, but she just didn't have the vocabulary to be indirect about it."

"She lost face at the office."

"In a big way." I concluded.

The contrast here is that Western face loss owing to others' dress is usually a matter of conflicting taste. "I am not going unless you change that shirt," is more common among intimates—as we often consider them to be extensions of ourselves—than with those we interact with on less personal levels.

As long as we are dressed appropriately for the situation, we are not generally concerned with the attire of others. Any ridicule is likely to focus on them alone. The Western concept of face tends to focus on the individual, while Asians are more concerned with the group. We tend to look at the way we present ourselves publicly as a matter of individual choice. In Asian societies, an individual's public face reflects on all with whom that individual interacts. As a result, one is always obliged to "put on one's best face" in public.

"Putting on one's best face," accounts for the strong dislike of showing emotions in public that pervades among Asians. If you lose your temper in class, you will lose face with your students for displaying an unprofessional lack of control. Physical control is also important, and the image of the ranting Westerner waving his or her arms around and jumping up and down in uncontrolled fury is extremely humorous to many Asians who rarely have the chance to see such behavior outside of the zoo (or maybe the market).

This is not to say that Asians can maintain control of themselves at all times. Keeping one's composure day-in and day-out can be taxing. Occasionally, people simply explode. This can sometimes lead to acts of extreme violence. Generally, in Asian societies, being angry enough to lose one's temper equals being angry enough to fight, and getting angry enough to fight could mean getting angry enough to kill. Fortunately, most Asians seek safer ways of venting stress.

Besides individual actions, individual achievements, or even the associated trappings, can also reflect on the group. A teacher in Asia can gain much face for himself and his school by hanging his Harvard diploma over his desk. Visitors will often pay more attention to the diploma than to the teacher. Nevertheless, the diploma, and the accompanying graduate, always reflect very well on the school and its administrators.

Asians prize education as a face-gaining instrument far more than Westerners do. Yet this concern for education is often more focused on the trappings of education than on the actual knowledge it confers.

A diploma from a university greatly increases the face of an individual, parents, and coworkers—even more so if that diploma is from a Western school. A degree from a well-known Western school is the goal that many parents encourage, and the wishes of parents are often a student's primary motivation to excel in school. The student's personal goals take a back seat or are not considered. While the majority of Western university-age students choose their own path when there is a conflict with parents regarding academic goals, very few Asians do.

Once the diploma is obtained, the wishes of parents are met. In all but the most exacting professions, little attention will be paid by employers to how many of the skills learned in school the owner of that diploma has been able to retain or apply. The fact that the employee is a graduate of the University of Such-and-Such will be exploited as a means of face-gaining for both the company and the graduate, as was the Harvard night school diploma that the teacher so proudly displayed. After all, it is the name on the diploma (Harvard University) that is important, not the quality of the education.

Face affects the teacher in many ways that can be controlled and many that cannot. With experience, you will be able to recognize a situation in which face is an issue, and act accordingly. There are times, however, when things are not so clear-cut, and you may find yourself wondering who is actually giving/gaining/losing face, and why.

In the classroom, gain or loss of face depends on an individual's ability to answer questions and do classwork correctly. Correspondingly, teachers gain or lose face depending on the quality of their instruction.

In Asia, the poor performance of students could also result in a loss of face for the teacher by causing others to question one's effectiveness in the classroom. In the West, the blame for a student's failure will usually fall on the individual student rather than on the teacher. In fact, student shortcomings could be the fault of either or both. But in both cultures, who is held responsible depends ultimately on the viewpoint of the administrator—who is, of course, also concerned with saving face.

Face is often responsible for silences when general questions are asked of the class as a whole. Those students who may be able to answer the question often remain silent in order to dovetail with the majority who can't—or who may need more time to work it out. There is a face-related preference among Asians, when necessary, for all group members to be wrong in a harmonious fashion rather than for individuals to be right in a disharmonious one. If satisfying the teacher is beyond the abilities of the majority, then those few who can might well consider it a loss of face to do so. Fortunately, that can work two ways. When the majority prefers to speak out, the minority will follow suit. In conversation classes, where speaking out is essential, a precedent of speaking should be set as soon as possible by using one of the "get to know each other" activities discussed previously or another activity that you deem appropriate.

Outside of class, face-related situations frequently arise. In an Asian restaurant, if one orders a dish that turns out to be inedible, one does not complain to the waiter. Most Asians would simply pay for the dish and leave, chalking the whole thing up to experience. If one does complain to the waiter, someone is going to lose face. So who will it be? The waiter? The customer? The cook? The manager? The owner?

If we were to mix Western actions (making the complaint) with Eastern ideas about face, the customer would lose face by complaining to the waiter, and the waiter would lose face by mentioning it to the manager, and so on until everyone involved lost face. In fact, the complaint would never get past the waiter—unless Western management techniques were used at this particular restaurant. We can see that what we may have considered to be bad service, poor quality, or a misunderstanding, has turned out to be a face-salvaging operation by the waiter. Admittedly, this does not improve the menu. But it does, at least, shed some light on situations that many visitors to East Asia encounter frequently but find inexplicable. The issue of face should be considered when problems occur that defy explanation. Face is gained or lost depending on how well one can follow a course set by the group (the majority). The guidelines for that course are often only visible to those who are familiar with the sociological/cultural elements that went into its making, and those who try to follow an unfamiliar path are bound to get lost.

As on a forest trail, it is best to seek local guidance, or to slowly make one's way to the end through careful observation and well-considered trial and error.

A tourist or foreign resident could stay in East Asia indefinitely without giving a second thought to face. Just as Asian tourists in foreign countries tend to pay less attention to face than they would at home, foreigners are given leeway (at least by those who often interact with them) in matters of face. Foreign residents in Asia who choose to disregard the norms of a society and live an insular life may only encounter problems when forced to leave their psychological island and interact with the local population on its own terms.

The teacher, on the other hand, deals directly with local society every day. This is why a teacher must pay attention to face: Learn how to give it generously, gain it humbly, and lose it gracefully. The society will do the same in turn. Although learning how to "put on your best face" is a slow process, immediate consideration should be given to understanding the face-related concerns of your students in order to facilitate the learning process, and to make students' adjustment to the techniques used in EFL classes as painless as possible.

Face in Asia is not static. It adapts to changes in society. With rising consumerism comes a stronger desire for quality goods and services. Consumer awareness campaigns are implying that it is not a personal loss of face to complain about being cheated. Young people are becoming more sophisticated, and with that sophistication comes a new, more modern, and less austere, form of Asian face.

Western Teacher vs. Local Teacher

Conversation-based courses at language centers throughout East Asia use Western teachers almost exclusively—although some use local teachers for the lowest levels. In some countries, universities use foreigners with undergraduate degrees to teach those who are not majoring in English. The English majors are taught by the local teachers and a small group of foreigners who hold advanced degrees.

Western teachers are needed at language centers because the conversational (speaking) ability among Asians who have not lived abroad is markedly low (Singapore, Malaysia, Hong Kong, and the Philippines are exceptions, as English is widely spoken in these places, although it is not always of a high standard). There are not enough competent local teachers to match the demand at language centers. Many individuals capable of teaching hold more lucrative jobs and are therefore not interested in it.

Students study English for a variety of reasons. In some universities and high schools, it is not a matter of choice. The courses are required. Whether or not the student is happy with a Western teacher in these situations depends on the student's outlook. The majority of low-level students (who are the majority of the students who take these courses) prefer a local teacher because they feel that a compatriot can give clearer instruction and, thereby, better prepare them to pass the exams.

In some cases, that might well be true. Local teachers who are competent in English can explain problem areas more clearly than the average foreign teacher. In other cases, when the teacher is only marginally competent, it is the blind leading the blind. Individuals from a similar linguistic background tend to make the same mistakes. These mistakes are reinforced continually, and they eventually become ingrained. If a student has been told to "join with" other students for his or her entire academic life, that student is not going to pay much attention to a Western teacher who insists that the preposition should be omitted in some situations. That student may also continue "opening" the lights or the TV forever. These types of mistakes are not always limited to non-native speakers. I remember listening to an American teacher confidently explaining to his students (nurses who knew better) that "sibling" meant child. We all make such mistakes. I tend to criticize words that I don't like (I hate the word "chopsticks," but there is no alternative). That wastes class time. Inaccuracy is inaccuracy—whether it stems from ignorance or antipathy.

Types of Students and Their Motivations

EFL students generally fall into one of three levels of ability:

Low-Level

Teenage and adult low-level students are usually false starters (those who have studied the language but cannot use it). Young students are often true beginners, and they learn quickly. True beginners are eager while false-starters are somewhat stubborn. I find the former much more enthusiastic, and easier to teach, than the latter. Both groups are unable to form or respond to even simple statements or questions.

Beginning classes at language centers should be more of an introduction to "the system" used by the center than a class on "English." I use the same materials as other teachers, but I stress method rather than content. This benefits both false starters and true beginners; they are exposed to, and made comfortable with, typical techniques used in EFL classes. They are given the opportunity to make the transition to "active learners" and will be prepared for instruction at higher levels.

False Starters

False starters abound in East Asia. "Ten years," is not an unusual answer to the question, "How long have you been studying English?" asked of a low-level student. That student would probably have found it very difficult to both understand the question and to form the answer.

It is often surprising for beginning teachers to discover that their students who can't respond to "What is your name?" have been studying English since early elementary school. It is common for American high-school students to study a foreign language for a few years, pass the exams, and still not be able to speak it. But in East Asia, English is a required subject taught in practically every grade.

Since false starters have been the majority of my students, I have observed them in-depth and come to several conclusions.

1. False starters depend on rote memorization. They are unable to put these memorized words, sentences, and fragments to productive use.

2. Since most modern EFL courses require students to be versatile and adapt the structures taught to various situations, students who depend on rote memorization can have difficulty adjusting—and as a result, learning.

3. False starters often translate everything mentally. Words and usages that can't be translated are often ignored in favor of those, although incorrect, that correspond with their own language.

4. False starters often have no experience listening to native speakers' English. Something said by the teacher might not be understood, while the same thing said, often incorrectly, by a classmate is. "Photography" pronounced correctly is rarely understood, but pronounced incorrectly (with two syllables) it is.

Intermediate

Intermediate-level students can form and respond to simple questions and statements, but they cannot hold a sustained conversation. They are generally able to respond to questions in class and to do guided activities. They are still unable to adapt language taught in class to outside contexts.

High (Advanced)

High-level students are able to initiate conversations on their own, do classroom activities with minimal guidance, and adapt language taught in class to outside contexts. Grammatical errors are still frequent, and sustained conversations can still be difficult outside of class.

New students can often be accurately placed when they register for courses by their responses to simple questions such as, "How are you?" A low-level student would not respond. An intermediate-level student would give a rote response such as, "Fine, thank you, and you?" A high-level student might say, "Great. How about you?"

High-level students often prefer teachers who are native speakers of English. They have advanced to the point that they are genuinely interested in the language. They are not taking the course merely to pass exams or out of some unrealistic compulsion. They realize that a native speaker can present the language to them more "naturally" and accurately. These students often have less patience than lower-level students with teacher mistakes and they are often quite familiar with grammar, grammatical terminology at least. Correct usage is another matter.

Some on the upper level study more out of habit than enthusiasm. Their teachers often find that it is very difficult to hold their interest. They frequently act as though they have heard it all before (which, perhaps, some have). You must work all the harder to prepare productive and entertaining activities for them.

At all levels, students expect, and deserve, to learn what is appropriate for their ability. The content of low-level courses should be checked and inappropriate material weeded out. High-level material must not sound condescending, and should be checked to ensure that it doesn't. If you have any doubts about what is or is not appropriate at any level, confer with other teachers.

In the average, mixed teenager/adult, low-level class, a desire to improve in English is not always the primary reason for enrollment. Mere curiosity, or lack of anything better to do may be the only motives. A very common answer to, "Why do you want to study English?" is, "Because my friend wanted me to."

Some adult students enroll with the specific intention of acquiring vocabulary related to their jobs, without realizing that it can take several years to learn to use it effectively. Some students sign up because they think a foreigner's class will be somehow dramatically unlike a local's. Others want access to a native speaker for other specific reasons, and tend to take up class time asking about unrelated topics.

People also enroll to take a "crash course" in English before a trip abroad. Occasionally, a student wants to meet a foreigner for personal reasons. It is not unheard of in Asia (or anywhere for that matter) to include foreigners in one's circle as a means of social climbing.

The majority of students who enroll in conversation courses are low-level, and the majority of these drop out before reaching the higher levels. Many of these students expect to "learn" English in a matter of weeks or months, often because advertising has led them to believe that they can. Interest often wanes when they realize how long the road to fluency actually is.

Special Courses for Children

Children's programs can sometimes offer comprehensive low- to high-level courses (often lasting a couple of years). These programs are successful from both a business and academic standpoint because children acquire language more easily than adults. The wide variety of levels offered insures that the child will be properly placed, and decisions to re-enroll are made by parents committed to seeing their children finish the courses.

Hess Language School, with about 20 branches throughout Taiwan, offers an excellent children's program in which Western/local teacher teams are used. Hess recruits both in Taiwan and in the United States. (Address U.S. inquiries to Hess Language School, c/o Mr. Donald Hess, 105 Lower Dix Ave., Glen Falls, NY 12804.)

Challenging Teaching Situations

Team Teaching

Children's courses (and even a few adult courses) are sometimes taught by local/foreign teacher teams as students are often quite young (five years old) when they begin. These team arrangements can work well if the program requires both teachers to be in class at the same time, and clearly defines their roles. The task of the local teacher in team situations is not merely to act as a translator. Local teachers are far better at maintaining discipline, and they are often better at certain aspects of teaching children (singing songs, in my case) than even a well-informed foreigner.

(Being conversant in Chinese, I once taught a class of very young children alone, for higher pay, in a school where this had never been done. The little darlings walked all over me.)

Some schools have local and foreign teachers in class on alternate days, often in an effort to reduce payroll expenses. This is rife with problems unless the syllabus is very detailed, and followed to the letter by both teachers. Another approach is to have the foreign teacher in every other class and the local teacher in all classes. This seems to work well except that the foreign teacher is often seen by students as a visitor instead of a teacher.

Mixed Age and Mixed Levels

Some language centers can offer comprehensive courses for mixed groups of children, teenagers, and adults, where the students' level is determined by a written test. If their score is high enough, they are interviewed and placed in an upper level. There is a strong interest among the lower-level students to progress to the higher levels, and many of them begin at the lowest level and progress to the highest in a few years.

In order to be able to offer this kind of course, a language center must have hundreds (or thousands) of students every term (to ensure sufficient enrollment to be able to open classes at the next level of progress), and there must be a set syllabus in order to maintain continuity among levels. Many smaller schools also try to offer this kind of program because the income from re-enrollment is attractive. But in many cases, these schools do not have enough students to keep every level open for every term. This results in misplaced—and disappointed— students who do not re-enroll. These schools often end up opening a few classes every term in which the levels are roughly set at beginning, intermediate, and advanced. The smallest schools will sometimes group all students together in mixed-level classes that will definitely leave students looking for an alternative school the next term.

Mixed-age groups are far easier to teach than mixed levels. In mixed-age groups, the children are often more receptive than the adults—leaving the children helping their elders. Surprisingly, many adults cope well with this role reversal (they may see their willingness to be helped as a means of "giving face" to the younger students), although some more traditionally minded older adults may feel uncomfortable and gracefully bow out.

In mixed levels, no matter what remedy is tried, one is always left with bored upper-level students or uncomprehending lower-level students. In large cities, students attend these schools once, usually as a result of false advertising or low tuition. The teacher will generally see a new crop of students every term. In small towns, where there may be only one language center, the teacher and students are left to work with what they have. This can be accomplished by breaking the students up into groups according to level and teaching those groups—at their own level—a common topic to be presented by the group at the end of class. This amount of effort, by the students and the teacher, should only be exerted if there is no alternative venue for the students or the teacher.

The most extreme level-mixing that I have ever experienced was in a language center in Hong Kong where I taught twice during the early stages of my career. The class was three hours long with students entering and leaving every hour. Some studied for one hour, others for two, and so on, making it impossible to teach. Once something got started, half of the students would have to leave, and more would come in. It is amazing that in a city that affluent, and with a reasonably wide choice of language centers, something that shoddy can remain open.

The Student Who Knows Everything

Eventually, you are bound to encounter a student in an advanced class who has "already learned English." These students talk far more than they listen (if they listen at all). They cannot be told anything new, and it often seems that their sole purpose is to "impress" other students and the teacher with their "linguistic virtuosity," though they are usually less fluent in English than they think. Students typically despise it when one person monopolizes the class, and their reaction is either to drop out or to stigmatize the know-it-all. In one of my university classes, one student was so obnoxious that nobody would do pair or group work with him. Nevertheless, he ran for class chairman in an "election speech" activity. No one voted for him. He was, however, mentioned by 80 percent of the class on the answer to an exam question that asked them to name the single worst aspect of the course.

Complaints

Although Asian students are not likely to complain about a class to their teacher, they do make their grievances known. This is often accomplished by complaining among themselves until their problem comes to the attention of another teacher or an administrator. The problem, which might have been easily solved had the teacher known about it, is then made public, possibly embarrassing the teacher, depending on the competence of the teacher or administrator, and the validity of the complaint.

Some schools provide evaluations for students to fill out at the end of a term. Student complaints on evaluations can be useful: "The teacher does not spend enough time helping students with class work"; "The teacher does not provide opportunities for students to ask questions"; "The teacher does not explain the purpose of the course to students."

Others can be inane, "The teacher speaks too fast"; "The teacher should tell students what will be on the exam beforehand"; "The teacher marked many things wrong on my report. They were not wrong. I just forgot."

Anyone with any experience reading evaluations can easily tell legitimate complaints from carping. Keep that in mind when submitting evaluations to superiors.

In any class, there will be a student or two who is simply incompatible with the rest of the group. This might be a serious person in a group of jokers, an older student in a group of children, or a businessman in a group of flight attendants. Once, for example, I had a very conservative Japanese businessman in a group of Thai elementary school children. After the first session, I suggested that he transfer to another class. Although he responded that he didn't mind studying with kids, he did not complete the course.

Another misplaced student who dropped the class was a high-school English teacher whose test scores had placed her in an intermediate-level class—with several of her students.

Because misplaced students are often the ones who have the most to complain about, it is advisable to persuade them to change classes (or levels) promptly.

Children tend to study in the early evening so adults should try the late evening; an early afternoon class will often consist of homemakers, while an early morning class attracts white-collar workers. (Although I distinctly remember a student in an 8 a.m. class in Taiwan who came straight from her job at the local fish market. It is safe to assume that the other students in that class haven't forgotten her either.)

If a change of class is impossible, teach to the majority. Your reasoning can be explained to the misplaced student. Many such students will be able to find their niche, and everything will be fine—as it turned out to be when I had a class of 17 children who were excellent students and one uniformed police sergeant who was below average. The first time he walked into class wearing his uniform and gun, the kids ran for cover, while I feared I was being arrested for some immigration violation. It turned out that he had no problems with getting help from the children, and he enjoyed the class very much. His uniform even provided a kind of realia for some sections of the textbook.

A very common complaint is that the teacher "speaks too fast." Students are often confused when they find themselves able to understand each other's English, but not the teacher's. This complaint occurs primarily because of a misunderstanding on the students' part. As we know, few people actually speak too fast; they speak naturally. Many students are unaccustomed to the speech patterns and syntax of native speakers. In Asian schools, contractions are often taught as elements of written English but not spoken—when the reverse is true—and you will find that students ignore contractions used in dialogues in favor of the full forms—just as they have been taught.

The request, "Could you speak more slowly, please?" should be expunged from every EFL student's mental notebook (and every EFL writer's teacher's guide) and replaced with, "Could you repeat that, please?" If you speak to your students in an unnatural manner, you are cheating them. Speak clearly, and pay attention to pronunciation and enunciation. Repeat as often as necessary, but never speak in a slow, unnatural manner that students will be unlikely to hear outside the class-room. The knack of speaking naturally and clearly without speaking slowly takes time to develop. Yet, once developed, it can be done effort-lessly.

Contractions and other variations of the language should be used in class by both the teacher and the students because they are a fundamen-tal part of "natural English." This can be demonstrated to students by asking, "Whadaya wanna do t'night? I'm gonna go eat. Ya wanna come?" (or a similar sentence in a form used commonly in your own country or area). When the students can't understand it, follow it up with a very slowly spoken "WHAT DO YOU WANT TO DO TONIGHT? I AM GOING TO GO EAT. DO YOU WANT TO COME?" followed by, "IF I SPEAK TO YOU LIKE THIS, YOU WILL UNDERSTAND LIKE

THIS."

You don't, of course, want to teach strong regional accents to students ("Hi thar! Ha y'all doin'?), but the general, natural speech patterns used in any English-speaking country should be taught and understood. The students will eventually catch on.

Below are the top three legitimate student grievances (according to my experience) in order of frequency:

Not Enough Time to Talk

Although common, and often the teacher's fault, this complaint can be frustrating because, even given the chance, many students are reluctant to speak. Still, this is the most common complaint in conversation-based classes. Many students feel that they are not really accomplishing anything unless they are speaking one-to-one with the teacher. In large classes, it is impossible to give every student that opportunity in every session. Teachers must rely on pair-work and group-work in order to give everyone enough speaking time (fully 80 to 90 percent of class time).

Students don't usually pay attention to other students during group and pair work. Ensure that they do by having them report the information they have received from their partners as a wrap-up at the end of the activity.

Students also tend to rely on reading by writing answers or reading each other's worksheets instead of speaking and listening. Cut down on this by having them use an upended book as a visual barrier, or by having them sit back-to-back.

Teacher Lectures too Much

This complaint is closely related to the previous one, and it involves too much talking in class by the teacher. All too often, EFL teachers assume that the role of a teacher is to "hold forth" on related (and unrelated!) elements of a topic in order to give their students a solid background. But students generally have that background and are now eager to use what they have been taught and experience its relation to everyday life. Structures taught in EFL classes are usually quite simple, and there is no reason for long speeches by the teacher. An entire class period could be used practicing something as simple as "I think" and "I hope." (Five minutes of explanation by the teacher followed by 50 minutes of related practice [dialogues, listening exercises, pair/group work] and another five minutes at the end of class correcting common problems.) Many textbooks are arranged so that entire units are dedicated to a few very simple structures, forms, and functions. The focus is not always evident from the material. Streamline explanations by checking the focus in the "contents" pages of the textbook and by informing students of what they should be concentrating on.

The ideal EFL class would have the teacher doing nothing except acting as a prompter and subtle editor for discussions that the students have developed themselves.

Student Teaching

One of the most effective ways to cut down on teacher-talk is for the teacher not to talk at all. Let the students do it. In high-level classes, I often assign each student 15 minutes (although it usually turns out to be much longer) as the teacher. I tell them the exercise they will teach, and the date, at the beginning of the term. They do their preparation at home. I help them by adding pertinent points to their "lesson," and they help me by showing what they (and others at the same level, generally) know. Student "teaching" is a powerful confidence-builder for students. Although the student usually painstakingly plans the lesson, the student-to-student interaction is spontaneous— another plus. By assigning different exercises every term, I have now seen almost every exercise in the advanced-level texts I use from the viewpoint of a student.

Few low- or intermediate-level students can act with much spontaneity, however, so the teacher's job is to work as a guide towards this "EFL Nirvana"—not to lecture about verb forms or your ideas about how badly people act at movies.

Plowing Through Material

When one simply reads the material and does not present it, one is plowing—a mistake often made by jaded teachers who are bored with their jobs. The students can easily detect this. There is a difference between using student-centered activities and tossing out material perfunctorily. Student-centered activities require the teacher to explain and monitor to make them productive. The teacher must act as an unobtrusive guide to keep students from going too far astray, while at the same time giving them a sense of accomplishment and control. Student-centered activities do not consist of handing a pair-work sheet to the class and saying, "Here. Do that. Wake me up when you finish," or, "Okay, what page are we on? Oh yeah. Well . . ." and just reading the book. The best guides can manage to seem very interested, to be nearly invisible when appropriate, to be there when needed, and never to let their charges go astray. Good English teachers also make good guides.

The Importance of Being Upbeat

After a long day, it is very tempting to plop into the chair in your evening class and stay there for the duration. Unfortunately it is difficult to motivate students from a chair. The more you get up and move around, the more attentive your students will be. This is especially true if they are also tired. Movement by teachers and students gets the blood flowing, the heart beating, and the conversation going. If students feel sluggish, get them up and moving by providing activities that require them to mingle. If you have doubts about the value of movement, teach a class sitting down, and then try one with a lot of movement. The difference is remarkable. Many teachers swear that a couple minutes of brisk exercise as a warm-up at the start of class does wonders for the attitudes of students. Others sing songs. I like to play games that involve running to the board or around the room (usually with young people). Being upbeat also includes using the right tone of voice and not slouching when sitting . If I hear my students talking to each other like 220-volt robots operating on 110 current, I shout "MORE FEELING!" and start a "lights! camera! action!" routine like a soap opera director (silly, but effective nonetheless).

The next section, "The Class," will outline what students expect from the teacher, and take a look at some more of the techniques and materials for productive and effective classes.

FOUR

The Class

Preparation: When to Draw the Line

The amount of preparation needed for a class depends entirely on how well you know the material. The minimum preparation requires looking at the material to be covered, and developing some strategy to present it.

Experienced EFL teachers can often do that without much physical preparation. Less experienced teachers (and some methodical old hands) tend to spend a lot of time working out a step-by-step lesson plan.

Both approaches have their pros and cons. Those who do less structured preparation are generally able to come up with productive activities spontaneously, altering their plan to suit the mood of the class. Lessons tend to go off on useful tangents when students show interest in a portion of the material that could take most of the class (and could be far more productive, because the students are interested and participating, than what was originally planned).

On the con side, minimal preparation creates the danger of getting stuck on difficult grammar points, or being unable to supply a correct response or explanation for an unusually worded or previously overlooked part of the text.

If, for example, you are required to explain the possible situations when "-ed" can have a [t] sound as in "talked," a [d] sound as in "studied," or an [ed] sound as in "started" you would probably need to plan.

If you have not checked beforehand, you might turn a page in a textbook and find something like this (as I once did):

Choose the word(s) in which the underlined portions have the same pronunciation as the first word:

1. cake   (a) station (b) water (c) narrow (d) small

2. cute   (a) chute (b) mule (c) pure (d) rule

3. feather   (a) break (b) cheap (c) great (d) ready

This type of exercise would seem pointless to most native-speakers of English. Yet where standard high-school and university courses contain similar material, you will be expected to teach it. Most native speakers would need some time to consider such questions and to devise a way to explain them before class.

Those who prepare carefully usually don't have problems with questions in the text. They do, however, tend to over/underestimate the time required for activities; something estimated to take 20 minutes may take only 5, and the (now unprepared) teacher will have to improvise. The topics/structures in EFL classes overlap a great deal, and those who rely heavily on preparation should be ready to put away the notebook and draw on previous experience.

Both methods of preparation have their limits. If you appear three minutes before class, pull materials out of a cubbyhole, and glance at them for the first time when you enter the classroom, you are probably overestimating the value of your experience. Your complete lack of preparation will be obvious to your students.

If you spend hours painstakingly preparing a conversation class (perhaps using charts, graphs, and maybe even a panel of independent experts) you are probably too enthusiastic. You will eventually be let down by your students. Over-preparation often leads to disappointment for the teacher, and excessive pressure among the students from not always being able to meet the teacher's goals and timetables.

The best conversation class has a strong element of "controlled spontaneity" and fun. The teacher can make an activity done a thousand times before look like something new and enjoyable. The goal of preparation is to provide a productive educational experience for students, and whatever works best for you in reaching that goal is the best method.

Using Extra Materials

Consider using photocopies of related activities not contained in the text or in the lesson plan that you have enjoyed using or have found effective in the past. If you do not want to pay for photocopies out of your own pocket, however, keep in mind that most schools using textbooks frown on the expense of excessive photocopying. In these situations, photocopies should be limited to an occasional class or shared by pairs of students (whenever possible).

If the course depends on primarily teacher-generated materials, then photocopies are essential. Nevertheless, it is still a good idea to watch costs by fitting as much on a page as possible, using both sides of the paper, and using the board whenever appropriate.

Some schools prefer (or insist) that teachers add samples of their own photocopied materials to a "community file" to be shared with other teachers. I steadfastly avoid doing that. The reason for not sharing materials is not (always) selfishness. Many teachers have a collection of "sure fire" materials that are the result of much trial and error; it can be frustrating to plan a class around one of those exercises only to have students say, "We did that last term." At the risk of promoting disunity, I suggest that teachers find their own extra materials and (quietly) guard them with their lives. There are so many EFL/ESL textbooks that extra materials rarely overlap unless they have come from the dreaded "community file."

Getting the Most out of
Equipment, Facilities, and Teaching Aids

Equipment in language schools consists of the ubiquitous tape player and extras like "language labs" and videotapes. Advertisements often show photos of happy, smiling students sitting in individually numbered study cubicles paying earnest attention to a teacher wearing headphones who is standing behind a sophisticated control panel. Admittedly, these ads make language labs look very attractive, but attractiveness and practicality are an infrequent combination.

Theoretically, language labs can be used for such things as listening to tapes, monitoring pair- and group-work, providing students with the chance to push a "call" button to talk to the teacher or other students, and other innovative activities, all of which can be done without a language lab (except the "call" button). One would think that a language lab would be an excellent place to practice telephone conversations. Unfortunately, many are not sophisticated enough to allow students to call others in the room. Students are usually limited to talking to a partner or the teacher. The use of language labs as anything more than a "high-tech" promotional gimmick or for student self-access—see Susan Sheerin, *Self-Access* (Oxford: Oxford University Press, 1989) is still mostly undeveloped in many parts of Asia.

Video recorders can be used to tape student skits, presentations and debates or to produce short video presentations in which the students act as writers, actors, producers, and directors.

Currently, schools use videos primarily as advertising gimmicks or to show English-language TV shows or movies. EFL-specific video shows are available, but are often so low-budget (understandable, given the low sales potential), and so badly acted as to be embarrassing. There are even some schools that use videotapes instead of teachers, which may be acceptable from a business standpoint, but certainly not from an educational one, as a student cannot interact with a video.

On the bright side, some EFL textbooks that incorporate video are coming on the market, and these appear to be a step in the right direction.

The various gadgets available at language schools can be useful if the teacher considers how they can best be incorporated into the lesson plan. Since it is unlikely that this equipment will be installed in every classroom in Asian schools (only one classroom, is more likely) the teacher must plan in advance to make the most effective use of it.

Video Tapes

Videotapes also have potential that, as far as I know, has been unrealized. A video tape "encyclopedia" could provide visual backup to topics in a text. If a textbook has a unit on travel, photos or illustrations of places mentioned could be put on an accompanying videotape. Many places mentioned in textbooks (the Colosseum, New York, Machu Picchu, the Hanging Gardens of Babylon, Altair-3, etc.) do not present the same mental picture to students as they do to the Western teacher. If places, people, and things could be seen on video there would be more consistency in the discussions of images.

In the future, computer-generated multimedia could incorporate aspects of computer labs, language labs, and video to furnish a truly interesting and productive learning environment for students, provided that the requirements of practical use take precedence over those of theory and advertising.

Teaching aids can be games, photos, props (realia), cards or whatever. Board games such as Scrabble, Scattergories, Life, and others can be used or invented. Photos, postcards, pictures from magazines, etc., can lend a visual aspect to the instruction. Props can help with lessons that involve operating instructions—like how to use a camera (or washing machine—bring one to class!).

A pile of index cards printed with various words can be used for many activities in class. A few sets of "Appropriate Response" cards are a must for every teacher. Cards of approximately the same number as students in an average class can be printed with questions (or statements) and appropriate responses (questions and responses on separate cards—one per card). The cards are shuffled, and one card is then given to each student to memorize. The cards are then collected by the teacher, and the students all get up and mingle, repeating the line they have memorized until they find a response. The students then confirm the match with the teacher, and sit down if it is correct. When all students have found their match, call out each question so students who know the answer can respond. If there is an uneven number of students in the class (Sod's Law again), two students can share a line to even out the questions and responses. If you have fewer students than cards, you can give the remaining cards to the first pairs of students who finish—they can reenter the throng to find another match.

All of these items can enhance a class if they are truly relevant and used with a specific purpose; a buffalo skull, a live tarantula, a picture of Ziggy Marley, or an orthopedic kneecap diagram may be your pride and joy, but some thought regarding its relevance is recommended before bringing it to class.

One of the most valuable teaching aids is a good basic knowledge of sketching. Sketching has myriad uses in the EFL classroom and is more valuable than a trunk-load of plastic vegetables (realia). The teacher who can draw well can explain almost anything. For those of us who are artistically handicapped—my students hold long debates over the identity of what I have drawn if it is something as simple as a cat—stick figures are the answer. A good book on elementary sketching can provide enlightenment on how to draw a stick figure correctly, and how to simulate various actions (running, sitting, walking, etc.).

Good Illustrations = High Interest

Asian students pay a great deal of attention to the artwork in texts, and comic books, primarily from Japan, are extremely popular even with university-age adults. Even the most boring grammatical patterns can be made interesting if the illustrations are good. Colorful texts are also preferred. (Some of my high-school-age students mentioned that book three of the Spectrum series [Prentice Hall Regents] had only three colors—books one and two had multicolored illustrations—something I had not noticed after seven years of using this text. A new edition of the Spectrum series has been published recently. All books in the new series contain colorful, well laid-out illustrations.)

On the other hand, students often accuse the Cambridge English Course texts of being too cluttered and over-illustrated. Collage-like graphics make simple things confusing.

In time, preparation becomes second nature. The bad chalkboard artist becomes a fair chalkboard artist, and a surefire arsenal of teaching aids for a variety of classroom situations is acquired.

Seating

The standard seating setup of rows of desks used in almost every Asian school is not appropriate for conversation-based English classes.

It isolates each row from the rest of the class and makes discussion awkward (it is very difficult to converse with the back of another student's head). Rows make it difficult for students to hear each other, and the formal atmosphere they signify detracts from the informal ambience we want to create. Semicircle seating is the answer. It puts everyone on equal terms, promotes informality, and eases interaction. By now, most language centers in Asia are using the semicircle setup, which is ideal for average-size conversation classes.

In small classes, a large conference table is excellent (these are supplied by the school; no need to bring one every day). In very large classes (in China, 150 students is a possibility) the teacher will probably have to keep the chairs in rows for part of the class period, and have the students rearrange the chairs into several circles for group work.

If your classes are held at a language center, the chairs will probably be left permanently in a semicircle. If you are teaching special conversation classes at a high school or university, the students will need to get in the habit of arranging the chairs before class, and putting them back into rows after class.

In some schools, the chairs are attached to the floor. If class size permits, seat students in a semicircle leaving the chairs inside empty. This is awkward, but it is is preferable to rows.

Generally, the teacher should let adult students sit where they choose, occasionally moving them around during pair- and group-work. With adolescents (and sometimes with adults) there will be a problem with mixing of genders. It is likely that boys and girls will segregate themselves in the separate halves of the semicircle, with a gap of as many chairs as possible between them. There may even be open hostility—this can vary a great deal among countries.

Most countries have coeducational schools, but some do not have many coeducational classes. In some (Taiwan, for example), contact between genders among high-school-age students at school is not encouraged, and it is sometimes even forbidden. (If you see a group of male and female students [in uniform] talking on the street—all with their right hand on their heart, they are not having a mass heart attack or pledging allegiance to something—but are hiding their name and student number from prying eyes.) All language centers are coeducational, of course, and the teacher will need to make some attempt at integration for practical reasons. It is more interesting for students if pair- and group-work partners are changed frequently, and many other kinds of activities require students to elicit responses from as many people as possible. Variety is reduced significantly if the only contact between genders consists of insults screamed across the room. This does not have to be a primary consideration unless it is necessary for the successful conduct of the class—such as during the activities mentioned above. It is not the role of an English teacher to press foreign social values on students.

Gender-mixing can be made into a game by preparing a set of name cards and choosing (or having the students choose) randomly for pair-work partners (appropriate response cards can also be used for this purpose). This method of name selection also works well for activities presented in front of the class, and prevents a student from feeling singled out by the teacher. If you can find a blank set of playing cards, the names can be written with an erasable marking pen and wiped off after the term. Playing cards can be shuffled and mixed far more easily than index cards.

Unlike children (who don't like to sit together because of . . . well . . . cooties), adults can be hesitant to mix because of simple shyness. They often appreciate being "forced" into mixed-partner situations and will be more than willing to cooperate. I have successfully played the role of matchmaker many times in my career by assigning pair-work partners who I thought might be right for each other.

A final consideration when arranging seating is that students copy each other's written work continually. Trying to stop a tradition that is as firmly entrenched as this is futile. There should be little written work in standard conversation classes, and what there is will often be done in pairs or groups anyway. Let students help each other.

For tests and exams in universities, high schools, and some language centers, the seats are arranged in standard rows with as wide a space as possible between them. Students know the significance of this seating arrangement, and will generally keep their eyes to themselves. Nonetheless, cheating on exams is just as common in Asia as it is anywhere else. Be prepared for mediocre cheating methods that are occasionally spiced with the truly inspired (like the infamous Chinese university student who spent hundreds of hours micro-engraving the answers to an exam on his pencil).

Opinion in the Classroom

Opinion-generating activities are a mainstay of many ESL/EFL textbooks. Getting students to express, defend, and debate personal opinions is a tried-and-true teaching technique that can produce very satis-factory results—*except* in East Asia. Most activities that require the expression of strong opinion do not go over well with Asian students. Public expression of strong personal opinion is frowned upon in most Asian societies. This is a source of frustration for many teachers from societies in which one's personal opinion is one's most valued posses-sion. In group-oriented societies, however, opinions are regulated by one's peer group and one's sphere of experience. While a Western stu-dent may hold strong opinions about a topic that is not relevant to his or her studies, and about which he or she has very limited direct experi-ence, many Asians concentrate entirely on the immediate topic. They do not often venture out of the parameters determined by their place in society. The standard answer to, "What would you do if . . .?" is, "I don't know because I've never done it." There is an increasing chance, as Asians gain more exposure to international issues and life in Asia becomes more influenced by Western values, that a carefully chosen opinion-based activity will work. But be prepared to drop these activi-ties quickly if they don't, as is more often the case.

Activities that require students to "Take a Stand" (see: L. G. Alexander, *Take a Stand.* New York: Longman, 1983) occur frequently in EFL/ESL texts written for Europeans. In Asia, these activities need to be reorganized to stand a chance of success. The best way to ensure expression of an opinion is to present topics that conform to a consen-sus. "Should men do the same amount of housework as women?" will receive strong choruses of "Yes" from the females, and "No!" from the males. The next step is to ask "Why?" and have them work on answers in groups or pairs (I try to arrange mixed female/male pairs for that one). The point of this activity is to get students to express any opinion. The "correctness" of that opinion is irrelevant. If you ask questions like, "Can capitalism and environmentalism coexist?" you will be met with silence—even if you take (waste) the time to explain the question.

One type of opinion-centered activity that does work is often ne-glected by EFL/ESL texts: "perceptual opinion."

Perceptual opinion activities involve language structures related to how one perceives data. "What do you think this is?" "What do you think ASEAN stands for?" "What do you think this is for?" "What do you think this means?" are all commonly used questions that ask for an opinion. Ink blots, sketches, strange pictures, metaphors, unusual objects, abbreviations, proverbs, affixes, and acronyms can all be used to elicit questions and answers that involve opinion that has no stigma attached.

Creative Classroom Activities and Other Wishful Thinking

There is a wide variety of activities in textbooks available to the EFL teacher, some of which are useful in East Asia, depending on the students and their general level of creativity.

Some activities can be salvaged by using group-work instead of the recommended pair-work; role substitution instead of role plays; songs instead of drills. Many activities in texts are valuable in content but not viable when it comes to presentation. Some course outlines require the use of painfully boring material. But good presentation can make the most boring activities useful and entertaining. The following list covers some common methods of presenting classwork:

Pair-Work

Most people feel silly speaking a foreign language to others with whom they share a common first language. This embarrassment takes time for some students to overcome. Help the process along by gently and humorously insisting that students speak only English. I have tried everything from continuously wandering around the room saying "Only English!" to charging a small fine (to be used later for a class party) to those who revert to their first language during pair-work exercises. Eventually, the students catch on. Any exercise can be done in pairs. The rule here is to get students to speak English when doing the activity. Students always engage in some native-language discussion before getting started. These pre-activity discussions help students get organized, so I don't discourage them.

Typical pair-work activities are the "information gap" type in which students are given "A" and "B" sheets with essential information missing on each sheet that can be supplied by the other student in the pair. Any exercise can be transformed into an information gap by using a bottle of correction fluid and a copy machine.

An unusual variation requires students to do a pair-work activity (short ones are easier on the ears) with the student sitting one person away from them. This activity is necessarily loud and is a very good way to induce students to speak up.

Other pair-work exercises could be interviews, role plays, dialogue readings, or simply working together to find the answers to a set of questions.

Group-Work

Group-work has the same goals as pair-work, though group work is especially useful for questions which have many different answers, or for simple exercises that would be completed too quickly if done only in pairs.

Dialogues

Dialogues are one method to get students to speak English even if they don't understand it. Students like them because they provide a way to "talk" to each other in English for extended periods with few mistakes. They are valuable because they introduce new vocabulary and structures along with examples of how they are used. The problem with dialogues is that students often read them with their faces in the book, and they sound about as natural as the digital woman who nags about keys being left in the ignition of some cars. This is easily remedied (although it took me years to find out) by "interactive reading." Interactive reading requires students not to look at the book when they are speaking or listening. They can look at the text only during pauses in conversation. When they are speaking or listening, they should look at each other's *faces* (not at the ceiling or at the teacher). The difference is astounding. It is impossible to talk to someone face-to-face and not be animated. The teacher should spring interactive reading on students after a few class periods of "normal" reading and use it for most dialogue and pair-work activities thereafter. Even students notice the difference. After a few class periods, they start covering up each other's books and joking when their partner takes a peek. Use this method religiously. It is one of the best. (Note that group dialogues are very difficult to do in this manner, so go easy on the students).

Task Listening

No taped dialogue should be played with the books open the first time. Make a set of questions for each dialogue and write them on the board so the students will have reason to listen. Questions should be varied and rather simple. Students have a difficult time grasping the main ideas of long dialogues, and detailed questions often prove much too hard to answer. Questions should be varied in order to stress certain aspects of the dialogue and to keep the students interested.

Information questions
Questions that are answered directly in the dialogue.
Either general, "What are they talking about?" or specific,
"What time is Steve going to meet Anne?"

Cloze questions
Leave blanks for students to fill in.
"Hi Steve! _____ today?"

Implied questions
Questions in which the answer is not directly stated in the dialogue.

Opinion questions
Questions asking what students think about someone or something
in the dialogue.

Drills

Drills work well with low-level students. They do not mind doing
them—so use them when appropriate. Drills can be made more interesting by splitting the class up into sections, "going around the room,"
or by using activities found in *Jazz Chants* by Carolyn Graham (New
York: Oxford University Press, 1978). Although a drill is mainly a re-
peat-after-me exercise, it can also help keep students' attention from
wandering, and it provides practice in both listening and pronunciation.
Several drills that work well with low-level students follow:

1. The class is split up into two sections.

Teacher: Do you like to eat desserts?
Student 1: Yes, I do.
Teacher: Do you like to eat deserts?
Student 2: No, I don't.

This drill can be modified for use with word pairs that have
minimal differences in pronunciation (snake, snack; lice, rice;
stripe, strip, etc.) with the teacher throwing in words at random,
and the appropriate section answering either "Yes" or "No."

2. The students ask the person next to them, and then the next,
and so on around the room.

Student 1: How's your brother?
Student 2: He's fine. How's your mother?
Student 3: She's fine. How're your parents?
Student 4: They're fine. How's your dog?
Student 5: It's fine.

This drill can continue around the room several times—
increasing speed with each cycle until the students can do it
easily.

3. The teacher calls out a time and adds a number of minutes.
Students take turns stating the correct time. This is done around
the room.

Teacher: 1:00 plus 20 minutes
Student: 1:20
Student 1: 7:00 minus 50 minutes
Student 2: 6:10

4. Tags—whole class.

Teacher: You're going,
Student: aren't you?
Teacher: You went to a movie,
Student: didn't you?
Teacher: She has two heads,
Student: doesn't she?
Teacher: There is more than one way,
Student: isn't there?
Teacher: That was good,
Student: wasn't it?
Teacher: You didn't come yesterday,
Student: did you?
Teacher: She doesn't have a book,
Student: does she?

Whole class drills can be done with any grammatical structure
that has a standard response. They can also be used to teach
pronunciation (tongue twisters, difficult word groups, etc.). If

the structure requires varied responses, the drill can be done around the room.

Songs

Some teachers, and many students, enjoy using songs in class. Most Asians feel comfortable singing, and even shy individuals will eagerly take part in group singing.

The problem with songs is that they are often chosen randomly, or because the teacher happens to like them. The teacher's likes and students' tastes will probably be different. REM's "Losing My Religion" contains some great grammar: "I think I thought I saw you try," but it is unlikely that the students have ever heard it. Likewise, although students are currently very interested in "pop rap" of the M.C. Hammer variety, NWA would not be appropriate music to use in class. With songs, it is best to choose the mainstream over the obscure. Students will expect the teacher to explain what the songs mean. I have seen several teachers attempt to explain "American Pie" to their students. Do try to avoid that kind of self-inflicted torture. Also, I recently heard Janis Joplin's song about wanting a car blaring from a nearby classroom. Ditto.

The best songs to use in class are simple, popular, and somehow related to the topic presented. Supertramp's "Logical Song" probably meets none of these criteria (except, possibly, the last, if you happen to be holding forth on adjectives and adverbs). Yet, it is a very good vocabulary builder—especially if students are given copies of the lyrics with the essential words blanked out. These can be filled in as a task-listening exercise for high-level classes. Many other songs can be made into grammar or vocabulary-based task-listening activities. Overly complex vocabulary and concepts can make these fun activities into a chore, so keep it simple in low- and intermediate-level classes.

You can also have students listen to a song and pick out the various instruments they hear. Choose songs carefully or this activity will be too simple. "I hear a synthesizer. Only a synthesizer."

Your advanced students can translate local songs into English, which can be quite interesting.

Role Plays

Role plays require the students to act out situations supplied by the teacher. East Asian students do this well because face is not really an issue when "playing a role." The only stipulation is to clearly define roles and to make the situations somewhat familiar to the students. You can assign short scenarios to be acted out spontaneously or longer skits that require some planning. These activities are often popular. Low-level students will probably need a while to collect their thoughts and work out vocabulary and sentence structures.

A good way to introduce spontaneous role plays to students is to prepare several short situations typed on strips of paper. Put the situations in an envelope, and have pairs of students choose a few to do as a warm-up. Give them time to think, and have them act out the situations in pairs. Afterwards, they can select one of the situations to act out for the whole class. Have the class guess what the situation is and answer other questions about it. These questions are usually necessary to ensure that the other students pay attention to those doing the role plays.

After the warm-up activity, call pairs randomly to choose situations from the envelope. They can then act out the situations in pairs, without preparation, and the class can, again, guess what the situations are. The following are some possible situations (I usually have about 30 to 50 situations in an envelope; these can, of course, be collected from the students and used in other classes):

1. You go to a restaurant and order an expensive meal for you and your friend. When the bill comes, you realize that you have forgotten your wallet.

2. You talk to your friend about a date with your boyfriend/ girlfriend. Your friend does the same. You suddenly realize that you are talking about the same person.

3. You are in a strange country, and you can't find your way back to your hotel. You can't take a taxi because you can't remember the name of the hotel or where it is. Ask for help.

4. You wake up in the morning to find a strange person sleeping on your sofa. Ask your mother who he is.

5. You are walking home late at night. You hear a voice out of the dark telling you to stop.

6. You see a good friend of yours on the street. You run up and say "hello." When he turns around, you see that he is not your friend after all.

7. You have lost your car keys, and you are trying to break into your own car. A police officer sees this and wants to arrest you.

8. You arrive at the airport to find that your flight to New York has been canceled. You are very angry because you have an important meeting—you will lose about $500,000 dollars in commission if you miss it. Talk to the airline representative.

9. You run into the car in front of you because it suddenly stops. The driver gets out. He is very angry.

10. Your English teacher tells you that you are on the borderline between passing and failing the course. Talk your teacher into a passing grade.

After the students become accustomed to doing spontaneous role plays, have them write out several situations to be added to the collection.

Other kinds of role plays are used in many ESL/EFL textbooks. Doing the short role plays above can be a good introduction/warm-up for longer, more complex types. My students enjoy playing roles of famous people in various situations, but they usually need most of a class period to "get in character." Putting familiar people in familiar situations works best. "John Pilger meets Pol Pot in the hallway outside Margaret Thatcher's bedroom" probably wouldn't work; "Mel Gibson goes shopping with Janet Jackson" might.

Role Substitution

This requires the students to play the role of another person: a celebrity, another student in the class, a friend, or family member. Role substitution works well because the students do not feel so inhibited and are more direct about their questions and answers. Have one student tell the class who he or she is (or not tell, and have the class guess), and let the others ask relevant questions. You can assign roles of historical personalities, but in order for this activity to be successful the students must be sufficiently interested and willing to research both their character and the questions to ask the other characters. If they show interest in a regular role substitution activity, character assignments can be given at the end of that class period for a historical role substitution class in the future. Tell students to research both questions for the other characters and details about their own characters.

Debates

"Debates don't work," is said often enough by EFL teachers in Asia. They can work—if the topics are kept reasonably simple: dogs/cats, love/money, co-ed/segregated schools, friends/lovers.

NOT euthanasia, the death penalty, abortion, and other such topics controversial in the United States. Give the students plenty of time to prepare, and rules should not be strict. The best debate I ever had in class was very easy to arrange. I told the students they would debate on the pros and cons of two local department stores. I then assigned teams and told them that I would neither give them help nor mention the debate again until the given date. They planned very well on their own and the debate lasted for three class periods.

Pronunciation Problems

Enough is Enough

By Rosemary Chen

Four letters cause me disillusion
OUGH makes phonetic confusion.
Four simple letters with four pronunciations
Make learning English tough for Asians.

OUGH has no logic and no rule
Or rhyme or rhythm; it will fool
All who struggle to master expression;
English may cause thorough depression.

I pour some water in a trough
I sneeze and sputter, then I cough.
And with a rough-hewn bough
My muddy paddy fields I plough

Loaves of warm bread in a row
Crispy crusts and doughy dough.
Now, my final duty to do
And then my chores will all be through.

My lament is finished, even though
Learning this word game is really slow.
It is so difficult, so rough
Learning English is really tough.

If a trough was a truff
And a plough was a pluff
If dough was duff
And though was thuff

If cough was cuff
And through was thruff
I would not pretend or try to bluff,
But of OUGH I've had enough!

(From *English Teaching Forum,* vol. 24, no. 2, April 1986)

Ms. Chen has a good point:
Phonetically, English is a rubber chicken.

We also have some difficult consonants. Ask your students, any students, to try, if they dare, this most difficult of English language tongue-twisters:
RULES
If they can say that, they can say anything. East-Asians have difficulty with "R" and "L" sounds—especially when they appear together (e.g., "world"). Final consonants should be stressed—especially the final "S."

Other problem consonants include: F, M, Th, and V. The following suggestions can be helpful.

1. To make a correct "V" sound, the upper teeth must touch the bottom lip. Asians often pronounce "V" as "W."

2. To make a correct "Th" sound, the tongue should be put between the teeth—with the tongue pushing against the top teeth.

3. To make a correct "F" sound, the upper teeth must touch the bottom lip after the initial "eh."

4. To make a correct "M" sound the lips should be closed completely after the initial "eh."

Pronunciation problems are often reinforced by local teachers who share them. Try to remedy some of them, without dwelling on the topic. The following tongue twisters could help. If they don't, the students generally enjoy giving them a try. (At this point, you could ask about tongue twisters in the students' language—some of those can be very interesting.)

This myth is a mystery to me.

My mother made me miserable by making me march to martial music many times.

Thelma saw thistles in the thick thatch.

Thin sticks—thick bricks.

A red leather lump—a yellow leather lump.

The little lad limps along a large well-lit lane.

Frightening Frank forced fearful Philip to fence furiously.

Phone Phil for fresh fish.

Students learning English also sometimes have a problem with vowel sounds in the words "walk"/"work," "dog"/"Doug," "snake"/"snack." Try these:

I walk to work, and eat a snake for a snack. My dog, Doug, dug ditches.

In lower-level classes, it is enough just to get students to use English to communicate. Too many corrections of pronunciation can inhibit the learning process. Corrections should be general (correct the whole class as opposed to single students) and pronunciation activities are often more successful if treated as a game rather than a requirement. Although I loved trying tongue twisters informally, one of the low points in my life was when I entered (I was coerced) a Chinese tongue twister contest. My tongue twister was comprised of the words "ten," "time," "business," and "be" (shr, shr, shr, shr, in four tones) plus equally difficult connecting words. I didn't win, and I certainly did not enjoy myself.

Topical Classes

Intermediate and high-level classes often focus on a topic rather than a grammatical point. Finding topics to discuss can be difficult. Students are not always interested in what the teacher thinks they will be interested in. Asking students what they want to talk about does not often generate satisfactory results, so the teacher is left to guess.

Walking into class and saying "Okay, let's talk about shopping," will not work. The teacher will need to provide suitable materials. These could include a combination of comprehension questions, pair/group-work, surveys, presentations, etc.

Materials for topical activities can be found in many EFL/ESL textbooks, and there are some examples at the end of this section. Keep in mind that a long, boring, reading passage used as an introduction or basis for a topic will quickly dampen any interest the students may have.

Introductory passages should be short and easy to understand. Any unfamiliar vocabulary in the passage should be there for a reason. The primary focus, in a conversation class, should be discussion. Topical classes are best presented in three steps: (1) the teacher introduces the topic to the whole class, perhaps reading the (blissfully short) related reading passage; (2) students do pair/group work, while the teacher circulates; (3) students present results to the class.

The following list provides suggestions for topics that *can* be used in class (Hot Topics); *could* be used in some situations (Controversial Topics); and those that should (in my opinion) *never* be considered (Taboo Topics). They are the result of much trial and error. Times change, and so does what interests students, so I have tried to keep this list as timeless as possible.

HOT Topics

1. Family and related matters: keep it positive and not too personal. "Who does what at your house?"

2. Travel: should be general—offbeat destinations will confuse students. Students often prefer group travel and conventional activities (sightseeing tours etc.). Keep personal observations minimal and related to the topic at hand.

3. Free-time activities: survey activities are best; introductions of offbeat activities (bungee jumping, toad collecting, rhinoceros beetle fighting) should be made if the teacher, or students—with the teacher's help—can describe them well.

4. Light superstitions: tread carefully, and do not make fun of anything. Refer to the sample activity in the appendix.

5. School: from the student's point of view.

6. Video games: any aspect.

7. Pop music: rap is popular at the moment. Teacher should know something about the local music scene as local performers are bound to come up.

8. Dating: keep it very conventional. The best way to do that is to use the activity at the end of this section.

9. Other People's Problems: the more humorous "Dear Abby" type can be used for activities focusing on giving advice.

10. Men and Women: (roles of)—nothing radical. Content should focus on students' opinions only.

11. Mysteries: students work together to find a killer, buried treasure, catch a bank robber, or whatever. See example activity in the appendix.

12. Social Customs: those of the teacher's culture, and those of the students'.

13. Inventions: common and obscure inventions —students can work together to invent something: a new animal, an exercise machine for a dog, etc. See activity in the appendix.

14. Food: recipes, giving instructions, etc. Recipes discussed should be local—or at least have local ingredients.

15. TV: discussions of, planning TV schedules, trivia questions about local shows (have the students supply them), mock game shows. Remember, most students *enjoy* TV, regardless of its inanity. Critical opinions from the teacher will be met with silence.

Controversial Topics

1. Social Problems: how to solve them, giving advice.

2. Heavy Superstition: ghosts, spirits, etc. Many students believe in these things; best limited to mature groups you know well.

3. Equal Rights: will work well with younger, more open-minded students. Avoid taking one side.

4. Environmental Issues: some groups are not mature/well-informed enough to be interested.

5. Plans/Goals: works well with some students; however, many high-school-age students are only interested in passing the university entrance exam given in most Asian countries.

6. International Historical Events: many students are not familiar enough with the topic to be interested.

7. Moral/Ethical Issues: not popular topics of discussion.

8. Raising a Family: younger students have given no thought to this matter—topic can work with older students.

9. Poetry: topic can work, but there is generally little interest. "Enough is Enough," works well.

10. Literature: generally incomprehensible to students and often not directly related to conversation. Best limited to reading/ writing courses—not conversation.

Taboo Topics

1. Politics: any aspect.

2. Religion: any aspect.

3. Capital punishment, euthanasia, abortion, and other morbid topics. (Mentioned again here because students complain so much about teachers trying to use them.)

4. New Age topics: students are unfamiliar/uninterested. If you touch on them, and students do show interest, be aware of possible conflicts with traditional/religious beliefs.

5. Sex and related issues.

6. Any topic that requires students to deviate from standard cultural mores, customary feelings of filial piety, or traditional ideas of ethics—the English-language classroom is not a place for instruction of that type.

A Realistic Class Schedule

Once you are established, and have a good reputation, you will be offered a lot of work. At that point, consider the following:

1. Working at a select few locations is far less stressful than running all over town every day. If you live in a large city, you will spend considerable time getting to class. Think about that before accepting an 8 a.m. class in a city like Bangkok—you

may need to wake up at 5 a.m. to get there on time. Private students should pay for your time spent in transit to teach them. Fifty-minute "class hours" as part of your teaching agreement with private students can take some pressure off if you have a tight schedule.

2. Students are often overzealous when planning private classes. They may say they want to study for two hours a day five days a week. This looks good to the teacher financially. Nevertheless, it is likely that the student's interest will wane quickly. It is better to think long-term, even when the student doesn't, by planning a realistic class schedule.

3. For most private classes, one to one and a half hours three days a week is reasonable. Longer classes become boring for both the student and the teacher. More-frequent classes often cause unforeseen schedule conflicts for the student. If you keep to a realistic class schedule, it is far more likely that the student will continue. The goal is to make class an enjoyable activity that the student looks forward to. Too much study quickly becomes a chore.

4. Allow plenty of time between classes when they are at different locations. If you have only 20 minutes to get from a class to another one across town, both classes will feel cheated. You will always have to rush out of the first class, and you will still frequently be late for the second class.

5. Start and stop class on time. Students have other commitments and do not appreciate the delay when a teacher loses track of time. This is especially true at universities where there may be only 10 minutes to get to another class across campus. Do not penalize students who arrive on time by waiting for those who are late.

6. If possible, try to schedule a couple of weekdays off. Many students like to study on weekends, which may be their only free time. Public attractions in Asia are often very crowded on weekends and nearly empty during the week. Having Tuesday and Thursday free can be very pleasant.

7. Be prepared for a frequent turnover with private students, and frequent schedule changes at schools. The English teacher who knows when he or she will be teaching, and how much money he or she will be making a couple of months in the future is rare. Established private language centers, universities, and private students with clear goals offer the best choices for those who like to work relatively set schedules. Flighty private students cause the most problems in scheduling. With experience, you will become adept at spotting them and either turning them down or referring them to someone else. If you are connected with a reputable school, you can request payment of several class hours in advance from private students. This might help prevent the student from canceling. Work at a language school or university as your major employment and think of private students as "extra" classes on which you are not financially dependent.

8. Be wary of accepting anyone for "intensive" courses before he or she travels abroad. These courses can be useful to some intermediate- or high-level students who only want to practice before their trip. More often, these students will be low-level, and there is little that even the best teacher can do to improve their English in a couple of weeks.

9. Keep your visa in order. Some teachers leave a country after overstaying their visa only to find that they are not allowed to return.

10. Enjoying the job is the key to success. After a few years, it is very easy to burn out. Don't expect too much academically; a frequent complaint made by EFL teachers in Asia is that they "don't teach." The job of the EFL teacher in Asia is to bring out and perfect something that the students have already been taught, and instruct them on how to put it to use. Keeping goals reasonable, and viewing the job from a clear perspective from the start can go a long way toward keeping it interesting for a long time to come.

There are English-teaching opportunities of all sorts available now in East Asia for anyone who has the right attitude, appropriate qualifications, an open mind, and a real desire to broaden one's sphere of experience by pursuing a career abroad. With new blood comes innovation—making possibilities for the English class of the future virtually limitless.

One of you may even figure out a good way to use language labs . . .

Appendices

A

Activities

Activity One: Do You Believe in Ghosts?

Level: This one works best with intermediate/high levels, although I have used it successfully with some lower-level classes because the vocabulary is not too difficult to explain.

Notes: It usually takes about two classes (hours) to finish this activity, and it could take three if the class is very interested, as is often the case. The only problems that I have encountered with this activity is that a few students have gotten frightened. I try to keep this activity as light as possible by concentrating on "movie" ghosts and monsters. It is essential that the teacher explain to the students that there is a difference, however vague it may sometimes be, between religious beliefs and superstition—and keep religion out of the lesson (be careful when explaining the meanings of "amulet" and "spirit" as they are both aspects of eastern religions; the two words are included because they provide a good contrast between the two. Remember that a "good luck charm" could be anything (a T-shirt, a rabbit's foot, a coin) and is not necessarily associated with religion. Again, this is a fun activity, but the teacher should remain neutral to avoid saying something that could offend.

Vocabulary list:

amulet	black magic	cult
evil	white magic	witch
monster	faith healing	zombie
good luck charm	ghost	herbal medicine
love potion	mermaid	witch doctor
palm reading	reality	sea monster
spirit	superstition	taboo
trance	vampire	voodoo doll
dream interpretation	omen	werewolf

Work with a partner and decide which of the above are superstition, and which are reality. Explain your reasons.

Activity A: Good and Bad Luck

In different parts of the world, people have different views of good and bad luck. Can you think of some others?

1. Some Americans believe that a horseshoe can bring good luck.

2. Some Europeans put strings of garlic over their doorways to keep out vampires and werewolves.

3. It is believed that if an Australian aborigine points a bone at someone—that person will die.

4. Some Japanese believe that catfish can predict earth-quakes by rising to the water surface and shaking their bodies.

5. Some Chinese fishermen will not turn a fish over when they eat it for fear that it will cause their boat to sink.

6. Some Thais believe that to hear a gecko chatter when they leave the house is a bad omen.

7. It is an American belief that knocking on wood will prevent bad luck.

8. Many American buildings do not have a 13th floor because 13 is considered to be an unlucky number; many Chinese buildings do not have a 4th floor because "four" and "die" have a similar pronunciation in Chinese.

Questions:

1. Have you ever seen a ghost? What do ghosts look like?

2. What would you do if you met a vampire?

3. What three questions would you like to ask a monster?

4. Have you ever been to see a fortune-teller? What questions did you ask?

5. Do you have a good luck charm? What is it? How do you know it works?

6. Do you believe in herbal medicine? What is it? Does it work? Give examples.

7. Do you know how to make a love potion? Do you want to know? Why?

8. What are the uses of a voodoo doll?

9. What is the difference between "white" and "black" magic?

10. Name some famous monsters.

Activity B: Dream Interpretation
Have you ever dreamt about:

1. being carried on a palanquin

2. seeing a rainbow

3. being in a boat

4. a nude woman

5. having a house full of rice

6. entering a new house

7. a tooth falling out

8. being put in prison

9. bathing in fragrant water

10. falling from a tree

11. killing a person who then comes back to life

Ask if your partner has had any of the dreams listed above, then work together to figure out what they mean.

(a) You will be hurt by someone.

(b) You will have a chance to be promoted to a leader's position.

(c) You will experience loss or unhappiness.

(d) You will be famous.

(e) You will suffer because of a woman.

(f) Relatives will come to visit.

(g) There might be a death among relatives.

(h) You will have bad luck or fail an exam.

(i) You will have a child of high standing.

(j) All bad luck will come to an end.

(k) You will get a job promotion.

Key to dream interpretation: 1-b, 2-a, 3-c, 4-e, 5-f, 6-d, 7-g, 8-k, 9-i, 10-h, 11-j

These interpretations are based on Thai beliefs; interpretations in other cultures may differ. Discuss differences with students.

Activity C: Ghost Story

Work with a partner to finish this ghost story:

A student was studying alone in a dormitory late at night. The other students had all gone home or to visit friends for a three-day holiday. The wind was blowing outside, and the rain was beating against the window.

The student heard a sound coming from the closet that reminded him of a dying animal trying to breathe. He could also hear a faint scratching like fingernails across a blackboard. He tried to ignore the sounds and concentrated on his book.

Suddenly there was a loud banging that came from all four walls at the same time. The student jumped up in panic and the banging stopped. Now all he could hear was the sound of breathing as the knob on the closet door slowly began to turn . . .

When you have finished, think of a name for your story and read it to the rest of the class.

Activity Two: Dating Survey

Level: Any level as long as students are able to formulate questions on their own, and are mature enough to enjoy the topic.

Notes: This format can be used with many survey activities. It is particularly good for topics in which the teacher's ideas may differ greatly from the students.' The teacher has no problem remaining neutral as all questions are generated by the class. The students should work in pairs to write the questions. When they are finished, they should then present the questions to other students in the class.

Dating Survey

Everybody is interested in dating. Now you have a chance to ask any question you want. Try to make the questions as clear and interesting as you can.

Remember, you will be asking your questions of the whole class, so be sure that they can be answered by both men and women.

Make your questions as funny and interesting as possible. An example:

> Someone that you like asks you to go on a date this
> Saturday. You say yes, and then someone you like a lot more
> asks you to go out on the same day, what would you do?

Activity Three: Breakdown in the Jungle!

Level: Works best in lower levels, but the situation and vocabulary can be adapted to suit any level. This activity is a good introduction to pair-work for low-level students.

Notes: This activity can be found in different forms in numerous EFL/ESL textbooks. There is a good chance that students have done something like it before if they are at an intermediate level. Low-level students often miss the point of the activity (working in pairs, coming to an agreement, conditionals, giving advice, the use of "should") and just run through it checking off items. The teacher may need to lead low-level students by writing the following outline on the board:

A: What do you think she should take?

B: I think she should take _____

A: Why?

B: Because if she takes _____, she can use it/ them to _____.

A: It might be better if she took _____, because _____.

B: Okay.

Students may have problems coming to an agreement; the teacher should stress the other points of the activity, and wind up by asking each pair or group of students why they have chosen particular items. The teacher will also need to explain that the items preceded by "a/an" on the list (first mention) should be preceded by "the" instead during their discussion. This can be explained by pointing out "a map" in the text and "the map" in the list.

Breakdown in the Jungle!

A woman is driving alone down a dirt road in the jungle. She is delivering food and other supplies to a remote mountain village. It is getting dark, and she begins to wonder if she has taken a wrong turn because she has not seen another car since she turned off the main road over five hours ago. She stops the car to look at a road map, but it only shows the main roads: the area that she is in is just a big, blank spot on the map. She puts the map away, and turns the ignition key. Nothing. After several tries, the car will still not start. She decides that she will walk back to the main road.

She has the following items in the car, but she decides that she can only take five of them:

a knife
a compass
a lighter
a small bag of clothes
a radio/cassette tape player
several boxes of canned food (one can is one item)
100 one-kilo bags of rice (one bag is one item)
A box of small first-aid kits (one kit is one item)
a toothbrush
a mirror
a flashlight
money
an address book with telephone numbers of friends
a news magazine
a camera
a pocket video game
binoculars
a small portable stove
candy

How long will it take her to walk back to the road? Which items should she take? Why?

Activity Four: A Difficult Choice

Level: Intermediate
Notes: This activity is always popular. It is a good way to practice giving advice and using impossible conditionals: "If I were her, I would . . .". I adapted this activity from the original in *React/Interact* (by Donald R. H. Byrd and Isis Clemente-Cabetas, New York: Regents, 1980)—not because there is anything wrong with the original—I just wanted a change after using it for several years.

A Difficult Choice

It is the year 3075. The World Government has decided that all marriage partners must be selected by computer. Anne received her list of choices 11 months ago. She has gotten to know all four men, and each one would like to marry her. She must decide quickly before the one-year deadline—it cannot be extended!

Background information on Anne:

Anne is the director of a company that exports Earth products to other star systems. Her position holds a lot of responsibility, and she enjoys her job very much. She is very active in her work, and she enjoys meeting new people and would like to continue working, but she would also like to have a family. There are things about each applicant that she likes as well as things she dislikes. She has asked for your help in making the decision.

John:
- a poor musician
- must often travel to other star systems with his band
- very handsome; has had many girlfriends in the past
- excellent health
- says that he is madly in love with Anne
- takes her to exciting places but she often has to pay for both of them
- has recently written a love song about Anne that became an interstellar hit. He paid back debts with the money.

◆self-confident, arrogant, and egoistic
◆does not want children now
◆wants Anne to keep her job

Yoshi:
◆a rich owner of a spaceship manufacturing company—
prefers to run the company from home
◆dignified older man—is 20 years older than Anne
◆has minor health problems
◆is very fond of Anne, but he is too reserved to talk of
love; has been married three times in the past; he has five
grown children
◆does not like to travel, but would not mind if Anne took
vacations alone
◆often gives Anne very expensive gifts
◆reserved and traditional ideas
◆would like to have another child
◆thinks Anne should run her company from home

Raymond:
◆the director of a dinosaur ranch on the remote planet
Jurassica 3
◆rugged, outdoor type—good-looking but not handsome
◆about the same age as Anne
◆good health
◆has told Anne that she is the most important thing in his
life—has had several short affairs—mostly with aliens
◆plans to live on Jurassica 3 for the rest of his life
◆has named a new animal after Anne—she thinks his work
is very interesting
◆would like to have a family
◆is not sure what Anne should do about her company

Huang:
◆a middle-class philosopher
◆handsome, but near-sighted—five years older than Anne
◆good health, sees a psychiatrist regularly
◆always talks of "the true meaning of love"
◆writes epic love poems about her; had one affair that
lasted five years

◆likes to travel, but only to hear lectures, poetry readings, and opera
◆gives Anne cute gifts that he makes himself
◆unable to have children
◆would like to adopt an alien
◆wants Anne to decide for herself about her career

1. Discuss the information about each man. What do you think Anne would like/dislike about each one?

2. Decide the most attractive and the most unattractive characteristic of each man. Why do you think as you do?

3. Decide which man Anne should marry? How did you reach your decision?

4. What would you do if you were Anne ("If I were Anne, I would . . .").

Activity Five: Design a New Animal

Level: Any level—vocabulary can be adjusted to match students' ability (This is based on an activity in *Idea Bank,* by Stephen A. Sadow, Newbury House, 1982.)

Notes: This activity works without fail; it requires no photocopies (vocabulary and questions can be written on the board), and the students truly enjoy it. The introduction is very important in this activity. In a low-level class, I usually start with a general discussion of animals; in higher levels, I ask about animal personalities (a dog is loyal, etc.). After a short discussion, I mention that I think the world needs a new animal, and it is the students' job to invent one—which they then do in pairs or groups. The teacher should emphasize that the animal must be completely new (no dragons, unicorns, etc.) and that the name is very important—and must be in English. The grammatical focus here is on comparisons, but the main focus is on fun and creativity in English.

Design an Animal

Vocabulary (these words are examples; the teacher will want to choose vocabulary to match the students' level):

carnivore	paw	wings
scales	herbivore	hoof
feathers	horns	omnivore
antlers	nest	fur
warm-blooded	cold-blooded	nocturnal
fangs	stinger	environment
habitat	claws	spines

1. What does your animal look like? (Example: "it's about the same size and shape as a deer, but it has blue fur, fangs, and wings like a bat.")

2. What does it eat?

3. What are its habits?

4. What kind of habitat does it live in?

5. What kind of sound does it make? (students must use comparisons, and give a demonstration).

6. What is the name of your animal?

Activity Six: What's Cooking?

Level: Low to intermediate—can be adapted to higher levels.

Notes: This activity is included here as an example of the many activities of this type found in EFL/ESL textbooks. The focus is on giving/receiving step-by-step instructions and the many related verbs. The recipes are intentionally very simple (and not exactly gourmet: according to my students). You should encourage variations/corrections. I have found that many activities of this type include recipes that are unknown to East Asians. Presumably, this is to provide variety. I have found, however, that unfamiliar recipes only tend to complicate things, thus shifting the students' attention away from the purpose of the activity. The teacher should allow two class periods for this activity.

What's Cooking?

Vocabulary:
boil
break
chop
directions
drain
favorite
fold
fry
ingredients
mix
picnic
pour
raw
recipe
sauce pan
serve
slice
stir
tablespoon
teaspoon

Questions:

1. Can you cook? What do you cook best?

2. Who does most of the cooking at your house?

3. Have you ever tried food from other countries? What foods did you try?

4. Do you think men or women make better cooks?

5. What do you usually eat for breakfast?

6. What is your favorite food?

7. What food do you like least?

8. Is a tomato a fruit or a vegetable?

9. Name some foods that can be eaten raw.

10. What are the best foods to take on a picnic?

Look at these recipes:

Fried Rice

Ingredients:

3 cups white rice	1/4 cup cooking oil
1 teaspoon salt	1 clove garlic
2 eggs	fish sauce to taste
1 onion	1 tomato
6 ounces boneless chicken	

Directions:

First, chop the onion, tomatoes, garlic, and chicken into small pieces.

Then you should heat the oil in a saucepan. Add the boiled rice when the oil is hot.

After that, stir the rice and add salt.

Then add chopped chicken, onion, tomato, and garlic. Continue stirring and add eggs.

Finally, add fish sauce to taste and serve.

Cheese Omelet

Ingredients:
butter
two eggs
1 slice cheese
2 tablespoons chopped onion
2 ounces milk

_____ break eggs into a bowl, and add milk and onion. Stir until mixed. _____, melt the butter in a saucepan, pour the contents of the bowl into the pan.

When the eggs are nearly cooked, place the cheese slice on top. Fold the omelet in half over the cheese. Turn over until it is cooked evenly and serve.

Activity A

After looking at the recipes, work with a partner to write one of your own. Be sure to put the directions in the correct order.

Name of recipe:

Ingredients:

Directions:

After you have finished, compare your recipes with those of your classmates.

Activity B

Part One
(Teacher should not allow students to see Part Two at this time.)

With a partner, choose six food items from the list below:

a loaf of bread
a potato
a pound of cheese
a cooked chicken
a large fish head
6 cans of cola
a watermelon
a pound of butter
a bar of chocolate
6 oranges
8 eggs
10 lemons
a box of cookies
a can of fish
a pot of boiled rice
4 green coconuts
6 boiled chicken necks
1 head of cabbage
1 large, cold pizza

Part Two
You are going on a picnic with four friends. You and your partner have been put in charge of the food. You must use the six items that you have chosen (no more, no less) but you can buy four more items at the store. What will you make? Use your imagination.

Activity Seven: A New Soft Drink

Level: Intermediate to advanced

Notes: This activity is adapted from a unit in *The Non-Stop Discussion Workbook* by George Rooks. The original requires students to design and market a new mouthwash—a less-than-exciting product. Most any product the teacher feels is appropriate can be used in this activity (or let each group of students choose their own), and the focus is creative pair or group work. Students should concentrate primarily on the name, the slogan, and the TV commercial. Teacher should mention some popular slogans to the class as examples.

A new soft drink

1. What is the name of your new soft drink?

2. What will it taste like?
(a) fruit, herbs, vegetables, cola, other (b) sweet, salty, neutral, sour, bitter, other

3. What kind of container will it be sold in?
bag, can, bottle, carton, box, other

4. What color, size, and shape will the container be?

5. Draw a picture of the label.

6. To what age group do you want to market your drink?

8. Where will you do most of your advertising?
(a) What kind of TV programs? (b) What kind of magazines?
(c) Name some other places you will advertise.

9. Create and perform a short TV commercial for your soft drink (every member of your group must participate).

10. Create a jingle or a slogan for your soft drink.

The following is a related activity that takes less time, but also allows the students to work together to create something (this activity is as close as I get to politics):

Design a Flag

You are citizens of a new country: Asiatica. Your president has asked you to design an appropriate flag to represent your country. Work in groups to answer the following questions:

1. What size and shape will the flag be?
2. Will there be any symbols on it?
3. What colors will it have, and what will each stand for?
4. Draw a picture of your new flag.

Activity Eight: It's Gone!

Level: This activity works best with intermediate-level students. Many alternative mysteries geared toward various levels can be found in numerous EFL/ESL texts.

Notes: The teacher should guide students to ensure that they figure out who each person is before they try to figure out who did it. If the teacher feels that the activity is too easy for a particular class, the clues can be cut up in strips with one or two clues distributed to each student in each group—this lends an "information exchange" aspect to the activity and also makes it a bit more of a challenge.

I usually use the code at the end of the activity if there is extra time (it can be written on the board) or I assign it for homework.

Work in groups to figure out who took "The Eye of the Elephant."

It's Gone!

Detective Nolock Homeless and his beautiful assistant P.D. Dames have been sent to the home of Colonel Edward J. Wimply to investigate the theft of "The Eye of the Elephant," a 20-carat diamond that Colonel Wimply kept in his safe. Including the Colonel, there were five people in the house or on the grounds at the time of the theft. The safe showed no signs of forced entry, and only the members of Colonel Wimply's family know the combination. Mr. Homeless has made himself comfortable in an armchair while Miss Dames looks for clues.

This is what she found:

1. Colonel Wimply has been confined to a wheelchair since he fell out of his staff car during World War II.

2. The other people in the house were: a basketball player, a mystery writer, a soldier, and the gardener.

3. There was a muddy footprint on a chair near the fireplace.

4. Colonel Wimply's daughter, Grace, is seven feet tall.

5. Mr. Trivialanian spent most of the afternoon arguing with his agent on the telephone in the study. He only left for a few minutes to find another bottle of whiskey.

6. Grace opened the safe for Colonel Wimply at about 5:30 p.m. to find that "The Eye of the Elephant" was gone.

7. Mr. Trivialanian was surprised to smell pipe smoke when he returned to the study.

8. The safe is located in the study behind a painting above the fireplace.

9. Colonel Wimply watched Stan tend the roses in the garden for most of the afternoon; the Colonel then fired him for being too lazy.

10. The soldier smokes a pipe.

11. Colonel Wimply's son, Ben, was hunting on the grounds at the time of the theft.

Work with a partner to solve the mystery of who took "The Eye of the Elephant."

Questions:
1. Who is the basketball player?

2. What is the gardener's name?

3. Who is the soldier?

4. What is the mystery writer's name?

5. Do you think the basketball player took the diamond? Why or why not?

6. Could the soldier have taken the diamond?

7. What happened to the gardener? Did he do it?

8. Did the mystery writer take the diamond?

9. Who knew the combination to the safe?

10. Who took "The Eye of the Elephant"?

11. How did he/she do it? Why do you think he/she did it?

A Secret Code

BM WOL MAS LHERBSK!

After you have figured out the code, use it to write some messages to your classmates.

[key to code: O-U=A-G, A-G=H-N, H-N=O-U, V-Z=V-Z]

Activity Nine: Language Games

1. Ladders

Two teams of students line up at the back of the room.

The teacher draws a ladder on each side of the board—the number of rungs depends on available time and the level of the class—I use 15 to 25.

One student from each team runs to the board and writes a word at the bottom rung of the ladder; that student then runs back to hand the chalk to the next teammate in line who then runs to the board, and writes a word that begins with the last letter of the preceding word. This continues until one team reaches the top rung. Points are added by the number of letters in every correctly spelled word. Misspelled words don't count. Stress that students must run all the way to the back of the room and they can't meet each other halfway. This game is best for young low-level students.

2. Categories

Students are put in groups of three or four. The teacher writes a category on the board for each group of students (fruits, vegetables, cars, countries, etc.). Each group must write as many words in their category as they can within a set time limit (I give them 2 to 3 minutes depending on the difficulty of the category). This activity can be made more challenging by randomly selecting one letter that all words in all categories must begin with. The teacher should plan categories of roughly equal difficulty in advance: if the groups were fruits, animals, flowers, and colors, flowers would lose because the students are much better acquainted with the other categories. Avoid unfamiliar categories (famous New Yorkers, British prime ministers, French movie stars, hockey players, etc.). This game can be adapted to any level if categories are chosen well.

3. Alibi

Although perhaps one of the oldest games used in teaching EFL/ ESL, it is only known to teachers who do their homework, so there is a good chance that the students will never have played it.

A crime has taken place, and the teacher accuses three students (I say my dog was kidnapped). The police have narrowed down the time of the crime to between 1 p.m. and 8 p.m. The three suspects imagine that they were together when the crime was committed. They must leave the room and discuss in detail what they were doing at the time of the crime in detail (unless the suspects are very advanced in English it is preferable that they use their own language to discuss their activities as it is essential that they all have consistent stories). The other students in the class will interrogate the students one-by-one about their activities and look for inconsistencies in their alibis. The teacher should coach the students in the room regarding the questions they will ask (if the "suspects" say they went to a movie, the interrogators should ask where they sat, how they got there, etc.). The teacher should check on the students outside to ensure that they are discussing their activities in enough detail, and be sure the interrogators know that they should ask each suspect similar questions. When both groups are ready, the suspects return to the room individually to be interrogated. The suspects should stay in the room after being questioned so they cannot advise the suspects who remain outside. When all three suspects have been interrogated, they should all leave the room while the other students compare notes on differences in their stories. Afterwards, they can all be questioned together so that they can attempt to defend themselves.

This game works best with higher-level groups who need practice in asking/answering questions (nearly all upper-intermediate groups).

4. Concentration

On a sheet of paper, the teacher draws a grid of 30 squares (horizontal squares labeled A through F; vertical squares marked 1 through 5). In the squares, randomly write 15 pairs of words or phrases—these could be pairs of identical words, pairs of synonyms, antonyms, or any other pairs that are clearly linked. This sheet is the teacher's key.

In class, the teacher draws the grid on the board excluding the words. The students are split into two groups; each group, in turn, calls out a square (e.g., B4). From the key, the teacher then says the word that is written in that square *one time*. The second group then calls out a square, and the teacher says the word in that square. If the word being called and the previous team's word are a pair, then the team that guessed the match gets a point and the two words are written into the grid. This is all done from memory—no note taking is allowed. Each team must call out a square in turn and only consecutively called words can make a pair. No matches can be made out of turn. This continues until the grid is filled in.

This game is very difficult to explain to students (and some teachers) the first time. The easiest way to explain it is to use a six-square grid as an example:

Grid on blackboard:

	A	B	C
1			
2			

Teacher's key:

	A	B	C
1	dog	fish	dog
2	cat	fish	cat

Team A: B2
Teacher: fish
Team B: C1
Teacher: dog
Team A: A1
Teacher: dog (Team A gets a point)

The game proceeds with Team B guessing a square, and continues until the grid is completed.

This game is very popular with all levels, and it is a very good way to get students to remember vocabulary used in the text or from a previous lesson.

5. Road Rally

The teacher prepares two sets of city street maps (A and B). The map for student A has eight places deleted, and the map for student B has eight places deleted; each map has a list of the 16 destinations. Students must sit back-to-back and, in turn, give directions to each place (student A gives directions to location 1 which is deleted from student B's map, then student B gives directions from location 1 to location 2 which is deleted from A's map, and so on). The first pair of students to finish wins the game.

This activity is a good introduction to pair-work and information exchange for low-level students. It should be used after students have studied "asking for/giving directions" (a section found in most low-level EFL/ESL texts) to practice the patterns studied. I have found that back-to-back seating works best with this kind of activity as it ensures that students will not look at each other's maps and it is easier to monitor than other methods (a book as a barrier, telling students not to look, etc.).

6. English Baseball

This activity is quite popular, especially in Northeast Asia where students are familiar with the sport and its terminology. It is best used as a review of material covered during the term and it makes for a good last class.

The teacher prepares a number of questions (about 100) and orders them according to difficulty: easy questions are singles, harder questions are doubles, difficult questions are triples, and very difficult questions are home runs. The questions should be the type that have only one possible answer. I put my questions in a small notebook with page tabs for each kind of hit; writing the questions is initially rather time-consuming, but they can be used repeatedly.

In class, the teacher goes over baseball terminology and splits the class into two teams. The number of innings can be decided according to available time (this game usually takes a whole class period). The students then decide (in whatever manner they wish) which team will bat first. Each student who goes to bat can choose what type of hit he or she wants until the team has three wrong answers (outs) and the next team is up. There are no strikes or balls.

The only problem that I have encountered with this game is that a team will sometimes ask for only singles in order to stay at bat for a long time. In that case, the teacher should introduce a "one-out" rule and/or a rule that forbids two hits of the same type being requested consecutively. It is better to state these rules initially rather than in the middle of the game (by the last class the teacher will know if the students are the "tricky" type). There is plenty of room in this game for personal additions (a way to use balls and strikes?), but the teacher should try it once as outlined above, to see how it works in practice, before adding anything.

7. Mind Reading

I use this as an introduction to a topical session on fortune-telling for intermediate/high-level students. It is an excellent way to introduce the topic.

The teacher must enlist the help of one student before class, and it is very important to choose a student who will not tell the others or act suspiciously in class. The teacher explains to this student that his help is needed with a game to be played with the class.

The teacher explains to the class that his great-grandmother was a psychic, and that mind-reading is a talent that every member of his family has (at this point, the students will boo and generally express disbelief). The teacher then states that she certainly can read minds and is perfectly willing to prove it. The students will, naturally, challenge the teacher to go right ahead and try.

The teacher draws a nine-square grid on the board and asks for volunteers to draw a picture of an object in each square. Be sure that the students know the English word for every object on the grid. When the squares are filled in, the teacher then tells the students that he will leave the room, and the students must choose a single object from the nine and think very hard about it (in English) when the teacher returns. The teacher will be able to correctly guess the object, and the students will ask to try again several times—the teacher will again guess correctly. Drama can be added by telling various students that they are not thinking hard enough or they are not thinking in English.

The student that the teacher has previously spoken with is the key: he has been instructed to place the top of his pen (or another common object) on an area on his textbook which corresponds to the square on the grid. Usually, about the third or fourth time, the students will attempt to trick the teacher by not choosing anything. The teacher's "assistant" has been prepared for this, and he simply does not put his pen-top on the book; the teacher should enter the room, very quickly say "that won't work," and walk out again.

This game is best for close-knit groups whom the teacher knows well. Again, the choice of a good "assistant" is very important. If one has any doubts, it is best not to try the game. (In the dozens of times I have used this game, I have only made a bad choice of assistant twice—both times proved to be quite embarrassing.) It is up to the teacher whether or not to reveal the secret of the clairvoyance. If the class goes quiet and seems spooked, I usually tell, but I don't often expose my assistant.

8. Review Questions

This is another game that can be used as a review during the last class, although this one requires that a textbook has been used during the term. It is the most popular game that I use, and a very welcome alternative to the standard reviews found in EFL/ESL textbooks.

The teacher introduces the game by asking "trivia" questions about the material covered during the term. Most EFL/ESL textbooks have characters or use specific locations to questions such as:

Where does Dave Jones work? How many people are in Jane Wilson's family? What does Steve Miller like to do in his free time? Where is Maggie's Flower Shop? work best for this game rather than grammar-based questions. Some specific vocabulary questions can also be used: What does S.C.U.B.A. stand for? What is a toga? can also be used. After the teacher has asked several questions as examples, the students are then split up into two large groups to make 10 questions of their own to ask the other group (this takes about 20 minutes). The teacher should stress that the answers to all questions must be in the book and that the team asking must know the answers to their questions. It is surprising how often they don't. It should also be stressed that yes/no or number questions should not be used because all the other team would have to do is say "Yes . . . Okay, No," or "One, two, three," etc. in order to answer those questions. The teacher should circulate in order to en-sure that the right kind of questions are being written.

When the questions are ready, each team, in turn, asks the other team their questions, which must be answered correctly within a set time limit (I allow 45 seconds). Books can be used, and the answering team can make as many attempts as necessary (within the time limit). If they answer correctly they get the point; if they don't, the team asking the question gets the point. The team asking must say "right" or "wrong" in response to each answer; they often need prompting by the teacher in order to respond quickly. The team with the most points at the end of the class period wins the game. If the score is tied close to the end of the class period, the teacher can give each team a couple of minutes to come up with a "super" tie-breaker question.

Afterward:
Other Types of Teaching

After gaining sufficient experience teaching conversation in East Asia, you will become qualified for numerous other types of teaching.

Test preparation courses such as TOEFL, GRE, GMAT, CGFNS, and CGFMS are offered in many language centers. Besides a thorough knowledge of grammar, teaching preparation courses for these tests requires a thorough knowledge of the grammatical forms used in each particular test: the British tests can differ a great deal from the American ones, and students also expect the teacher to provide shortcuts and tricks which will help them pass. Some tests (GRE and GMAT) contain questions covering a variety of subjects—not just English—and they are quite difficult to teach effectively, as the teacher has no way of knowing which questions will appear on the actual test. The most popular test preparation course in East Asia is for the TOEFL, an English test, which all foreign students who plan to study in the United States must take. A passing score depends on the academic institution's requirements and the level at which the student intends to study (most undergraduate programs require a score of around 550, and graduate programs require a 600 or more to ensure admission, although admission is possible at both levels at lower scores). Five language skills are tested in the three sections of the TOEFL: (1) Listening Comprehension, (2) Structure and Written Expression, (3) Reading Comprehension and Vocabulary.

The format of the test is predictable, but the questions will differ in every test. The teacher must know the test quite well in order to avoid going off on grammatical tangents that are unlikely to appear on the test. TOEFL preparation classes can be quite large, especially in Northeast Asia, and teaching methods differ from those used in conversation-based classes. Students expect to be given specific information that they can use to help them pass the test. Class participation is often minimal; however, a TOEFL teacher who can make classes interesting will indeed be very popular and, consequently, well paid.

English for Specific Purposes (ESP) classes are offered by most universities and some language centers. These courses require a knowledge of whatever discipline is relevant; techniques used in teaching conversation can often be used in these courses, but it depends on the venue and the syllabus. Many universities use foreign teachers for courses unrelated to English (world history, physics, or whatever); requirements and credentials necessary for these positions are often the same as in Western universities.

Lastly, schools which specialize in teaching English to young children are very popular in Northeast Asia (especially Japan and Taiwan), and these schools are also starting to gain popularity in the more economically developed parts of Southeast Asia. Many EFL teachers find working at these schools both professionally and financially rewarding: the students often progress faster and salaries are often higher than those for adult classes.

Experience in teaching K-9 students can be very useful when teaching EFL to children, and previous experience with adult EFL can make the job a lot smoother. One should also be prepared to handle the discipline problems typical in children's classes.

Some care should be taken when choosing a school: as a general rule, the large schools offer viable programs, while the small schools are often no more than glorified day-care centers, and the teacher no more than a baby-sitter (having a "Western English Teacher" is an effective promotional ploy). The small schools do offer competitive pay rates, so they may be a consideration for those who enjoy baby-sitting. There are more than enough large schools in Northeast Asia, and they almost always need teachers—due to high enrollments—so finding the right kind of children's school should not present a problem for those who are interested.

B

Universities and Language Centers

The following is a list of selected universities and language centers in East Asia. These schools are good starting points for a job search, and notice boards at some could be good sources of information on job vacancies, housing, local language courses, and used consumer goods for sale.

Japan

Aspect International Language Schools (AILS)
26 Third Street
San Francisco, CA 94l03
USA

Doshisha University Faculty of Humanities/English Dept.
Karasuma-Imadegawa Dori
Kamikyo-Ku
Kyoto 602
Japan

ELS International (branches in several East Asian countries)
ELS International Inc.
5761 Buckingham Parkway
Culver City, CA 90230
USA

Language Institute of Japan
4-14-1 Shiroyama
Odawara-Shi
Kanagawa-Ken 250
Japan

Meikai University Faculty of Humanities/English Dept.
8 Meikai
Urayasu City
Chiba Prefecture 279
Japan

Temple University
1-16-7 Kamiochiai
Shinjuku-Ku
Tokyo 161
Japan

Yamaha English School for Children
1714 Tatsuno-Machi
Kamiina-Gun
Nagano-Ken 399-04
Japan

YMCA/YWCA (more than 80 branches in Japan)
International Office (Asia)
909 Fourth Avenue
Seattle, WA 98014
USA

Taiwan

ELS International
59 Chungking South Road, Section 2
Taipei
Taiwan

Hess Language Center (more than 20 branches in Taiwan)
Mr. Donald Hess
105 Lower Dix Avenue
Glen Falls, NY 12804
USA

National Taiwan Normal University
Department of Foreign Languages
4F-10, Lane 54
Taishun Street
Taipei
Taiwan

National Taiwan University
Department of Foreign Languages and Literature
Taipei 10764
Taiwan

Success Language Center
10th Floor, Number 32
Liu Chuan E. Street
Taichung
Taiwan

YES
213 Fu Hsin South Road
Row 2, 10th Floor
Taipei
Taiwan

Hong Kong

Chinese University of Hong Kong
English Department
Shatin
New Territories
Hong Kong

City Polytechnic of Hong Kong
Department of English
83 Tat Chee Avenue
Kowloon
Hong Kong

Hong Kong Baptist College
Language Center
224 Waterloo Road
Kowloon
Hong Kong

University of Hong Kong
Language Center
Pokfulam Road
Hong Kong

Korea

ELS International
(see Japan listing)

English Language Training Center (recruits from abroad)
646-22 Yoksam-Dong
Kangnam-ku
Seoul 135-081
Korea

Jong Ro Foreign Language Institute
Jong Ro Ku
Kong Pyong Dong
55 Bungi
Seoul
Korea

China

Embassy of the Peoples's Republic of China
Education Division
2300 Connecticut Avenue, NW
Washington, DC 20008
USA

Embassy of the People's Republic of China
515 St. Patricks Street
Ottawa, ON KIN 5H3
Canada

International Scientific & Information Services
40 Thompson Hay Path
Setauket, NY 11733
USA

Note: A detailed directory, by province, of the major
schools and universities in China which hire English teachers
can be found in reference works such as *The World of Learning*
or *Living in China*. Letters of inquiry should be addressed to the
head of the foreign language department.

Indonesia

American Language Training Center
Jalan Panglima Ploim Raya
No. 100
Kebayoran Baru
Jakarta Selatan
Indonesia

The British Council
Jalan Salam No. 22
Pejompongan
Jakarta

ELS International (see Japan listing)

Executive English Programs
Jalan Wiljaya VIII, No. 4
Kebayoran Baru
Jakarta 12160
Indonesia

Hasanuddin University
Language Centre
Ujung Padang
Sulawesi
Indonesia

International Language Studies
Jalan Tanjung Duren Utara III A-334
Jakarta 11470
Indonesia

International Language Programs
Jalan Jenderal S. Parman
Kav. 68, Slipi
Jakarta Barat
Indonesia

University of Indonesia
English Department
Kampus U.I. Depok
Jakarta
Indonesia

Thailand

AUA Language Center (Bangkok)
179 Rajadamri Road
Bangkok l0500
Thailand

Note: AUA is the oldest and, perhaps, the leading language center in Thailand. There are numerous branches, which hire teachers independently, throughout the country. At the time of this writing, AUA Bangkok is preparing to change addresses.

AUA Language Center (Chiang Mai)
24 Rajadamnern Road
Chiang Mai 50000
Thailand

Chulalongkorn University
Language Institute
Prem Purachatra Bldg.
Phaya Thai Road
Bangkok 10330
Thailand

ECC (Thailand)
430/17-24 Chula Soi 64
Siam Square
Patumwan 10330
Thailand

Prince of Songkla University
Faculty of Science
Department of Foreign Languages
Hat Yai
Songkla 90110
Thailand

Silpakorn University
Faculty of Arts
Department of English
Nakorn Pathom 75000
Thailand

Thammasat University
Department of English
Faculty of Liberal Arts
Tha Prachan
Bangkok 10200
Thailand

C

Bibliography

Much of the material in this book is based on personal experience in the field rather than on secondary sources. There are, however, several books and periodicals that were instrumental in developing some of the theories that appear in this text:

General

Bennett, Gordon. *Huadong: The Story of a Chinese People's Commune.* Boulder, Colo.: Westview Press, 1978.

Coye, Molly Joel. *China Yesterday and Today.* New York: Bantam Books, 1989. A general overview of China and the Chinese.

De Keijzer, Arne J. *China: Business Strategies for the '90s.* Berkeley: Pacific View Press, 1992. An expert look at doing business in China—many aspects of which are relevant to life in other parts of East Asia.

Hartzel, Richard W. *Harmony in Conflict.* Taipei: Caves Books, 1988. Hartzel is a leading authority on Chinese cultural topics. He has published several books in Chinese in addition to numerous articles and columns in Chinese newspapers and periodicals. I consider *Harmony in Conflict* to be the definitive work on active adaption to Chinese society. This book is recommended for exploring some of the concepts presented in this text from a different perspective.

Hofheinz, Roy, Jr., and Kent E. Calder. *The Eastasia Edge.* New York: Basic Books, 1982.

Quinlan, Joseph P. *Vietnam: Business Opportunities and Risks.* Berkeley: Pacific View Press, 1995.

Reischauer, Edwin O. *Japan Past and Present.* Tokyo: Charles E. Tuttle, 1973. An overview of Japan and the Japanese.

Weiner, Rebecca. *Living in China: A Guide to Teaching and Studying in China, Including Taiwan.* San Francisco: China Books & Periodicals, 1991.

Useful Periodicals

English Teaching Forum: A Journal for the Teacher of English Outside the United States. Superintendent of Documents, U.S. Government Printing Office Washington, D.C. 20401. Short articles written by classroom teachers in the back of the magazine are often useful. Longer feature articles tend to be overly theoretical and somewhat tedious.

The Nation Junior. Bangkok: The Nation Publishing Company. A periodical published by *The Nation,* one of Thailand's leading newspapers. Although it is published for teenage EFL students, it is an excellent way to keep track of trends in Thai society.

Transitions Abroad: The Guide to Learning, Living, and Working Overseas. Dept. TRA, P.O. Box 3000, Denville, NJ 07834. Articles provide a good general overview for the beginning EFL teacher (or anyone wishing to live abroad). Advertisements and articles are an excellent source of contact addresses for volunteer programs, recruiters, etc.

EFL/ESL Reading

EFL/ESL textbooks commonly used in Asia:

Byrd, Donald R. H., and Isis Clemente-Cabetas. *React, Interact.* New York: Regents, 1980.

Byrd, Donald R. H., and Jason Mortimer. *Extensions* (series). Englewood Cliffs, New Jersey: Prentice Hall Regents, 1987.

Byrd, Donald, R. H., and others. *Spectrum.* Englewood Cliffs, New Jersey: Prentice Hall, 1983. A very popular ESL text series. Although this series is intended for ESL, it remains one of the most widely used courses by language centers in East Asia. The new edition focuses more on EFL than the previous one.

Gower, Roger. *Speaking* (Oxford Supplementary Skills Series). Oxford: Oxford University Press, 1987.

Graham, Carolyn. *Jazz Chants: Rhythms of American English for Students of English As a Second Language.* New York: Oxford University Press, 1978.

Hartley, Bernard, and Peter Viney: *American Streamline* (series). New York: Oxford University Press, 1983.

Jones, Leo, and Victoria F. Kimbrough. *Great Ideas: Listening & Speaking Activities for Students of American English.* New York: Cambridge University Press, 1987.

Molinsky, Steven J., and Bill Bliss. *Side by Side* (series). Englewood Cliffs, New Jersey: Prentice Hall, 1983.

Richards, J. C., and M. N. Long. *Breakthrough.* Oxford: Oxford University Press: 1985. A good three-level course. This textbook is unique in that it provides an interesting mix of British and American usage. The whole series would be improved if it were revised and modernized (the photos are from the 1970s). Otherwise, it is a good book for use in East Asia.

Rooks, George. *The Non-Stop Discussion Workbook: Problems for Intermediate and Advanced Students.* Rowley, Mass.: Newbury House Publishers, 1981.

Sadow, Stephen. *Idea Bank: Creative Activities for the Language Class.* Rowley, Mass.: Newbury House Publishers, 1982.

Seidl, Jennifer. *Grammar* (series). Oxford: Oxford University Press, 1993.

Webster, Megan, and Libby Castanon. *Talkabout* (series). Oxford: Oxford University Press, 1983.

STRANGERS ALWAYS
A Jewish Family in Wartime Shanghai
by Rena Krasno

A fascinating picture of the history and social life of the Jewish community of Shanghai in the period during and preceding World War II. Drawing on the author's personal diaries kept while she was a college student, and on extensive research, Krasno provides a personal, informative, and moving account.

Cloth $24.95

RED EGGS AND DRAGON BOATS
Celebrating Chinese Festivals
by Carol Stepanchuk

This beautiful book shares the experience of four of China's major festivals, celebrated by Chinese people throughout the world, plus a tradtional welcoming party for a new baby with readers from 8 to 12. Stories, folklore, customs, and recipes for holiday treats are accompanied by wonderful illustrations of festival activities, painted by some of China's best folk artists.

Cloth $16.95

LONG IS A DRAGON
Chinese Writing for Children
by Peggy Goldstein

A Parents' Choice Award winning introduction to the Chinese writing system, which takes the reader stroke by stroke from the pictographs of ancient times to the characters of today. Written for children ages 8 to 12, this book includes over 75 characters, including the number system.

Cloth $15.95

For a complete catalog, write:
Pacific View Press
P. O. Box 2657
Berkeley, CA 94702